Journey into Love

Journey
into
Love

Road Signs along the Way

Wallace B. Clift

CROSSROAD · NEW YORK

1990

The Crossroad Publishing Company
370 Lexington Avenue, New York, N.Y. 10017

Copyright © 1990 by Wallace B. Clift

Printed in the United States of America

Library of Congress Cataloging-in-Publication Data

Clift, Wallace B.
    Journey into love : road signs along the way / Wallace B. Clift.
        p.   cm.
    Includes bibliographical references.
    ISBN 0-8245-1032-1
    1. Love—Religious aspects—Christianity.   2. God—Worship and
love.   3. Psychology, Religious.   4. Spiritual life—Anglican
authors.   5. Psychoanalysis and religion.   I. Title.
BV4639.C49 1990
241'.4—dc20
                                                        90-35102
                                                          CIP

For my friends
at
St. John's Cathedral, Denver
and
St. Michael's Convent, London

Contents

Introduction

This book seeks to respond to the questions: Where are we going? and, How do we get there? It is about the human spirit and its growth and development. I write from a Christian perspective, but the goal as I perceive it (love) and the procedures suggested for how to get there (road signs) may be applicable, at least in part, from some other perspectives as well.

My experience as a student, teacher, and practitioner of religion and pastoral psychotherapy has led me to the conclusion that love is the creative force in the universe. Love not only creates, it heals and restores. Most, if not all, the therapeutic systems that I have studied entail some basic premise of the "acceptability" of the client. Accepting the other person, in their basic being, is the ground plan of love.

If we have a "purpose" or goal in life (as I believe we do), then it seems to me it must be to participate as fully as possible in this basic force of life. Hate destroys; indifference is not productive. We even come into being in the act that is called "making love." The difficult question to learn is: What is love? There are depths and then still more depths. I am still on the journey but think I have found some clues.

The nine chapters that follow are primarily based on the experience and insights I gleaned as a parish priest and later in my study of Jungian psychology, as well as the wisdom of others who have sought to describe the journey into love.

The suggestion of a movement or progress toward a goal is inherent in the idea of growth and development, and so one finds the image of a road, a path, a ladder, or a way as descriptive of the process in most traditions. The image of a road to be followed has been a prominent one throughout the history of Christian spirituality. Jesus is remembered as saying: "I am the way, the truth, and the life." Later, his earliest followers, as recorded in Acts, spoke of themselves as "followers of the Way."

The image of the pilgrim on the way of love permeates not only Christian thought, but also the thought of other religious traditions. In ancient Israel there was the image of "the King's Highway," and the prophets Malachi and Isaiah used the image of a way or highway of the Lord. Lao-tzu spoke of the Tao or Way, and Gautama Buddha of an eightfold path. Within Hinduism, there is the way of *bhakti* (loving devotion). Among the Navajo, the foremost officiant in the rituals of the peyote religion is called the "Road Chief" or "He Who Shows the Road."

The early church fathers and Christian spirituality throughout the Middle Ages found the image of a journey to be undertaken as their most common vehicle for describing growth in the Christian life. The actual experience of undertaking a pilgrimage has always been a vital and literal way of enacting one's journey toward God. The anthropologists Victor and Edith Turner in *Image and Pilgrimage in Christian Culture* say, "Pilgrimage may be thought of as extroverted mysticism, just as mysticism is introverted pilgrimage."[1] The journey can be expressed in both outer and inner ways. Dante's *The Divine Comedy* and John Bunyan's *Pilgrim's Progress* are well-known literary portrayals of the Christian's journey.

The psychology of C. G. Jung has been important to my understanding of the human psyche or soul and, ultimately, of what is entailed on the journey into love. Jung described his understanding of the psychological development called for in the human psyche as a "path of individuation." The road signs along the way are indicated in Jung's observation of the process by steps or tasks which are archetypal, that is, common to all who make the journey. My wife and I discussed Jung's "archetypes of the developmental process" in our *Symbols of Transformation in Dreams*, and we explored the theme of the journey in our *The Hero Journey in Dreams*.[2]

My analyst at the Jung Institute in Zurich, Dr. Jolande Jacobi, spoke of the path of individuation as a *Heilsweg* with the twofold sense of the German word: a way of healing and a way of salvation. Dr. Jacobi emphasized the spiritual and psychological relationship in Jung's thought. She wrote: "Apart from its medical aspect, Jungian psychotherapy is thus a system of education and spiritual guidance, an aid in the forming of the personality. Only a few are willing and able to travel a path of salvation. 'And these few tread the path only from inner necessity, not to say suffering, for it is sharp as the edge of a razor.'"[3] Jesus himself spoke of the difficulty of following the way: "For the gate is narrow and the way is hard, that leads to life, and those who find it are few" (Matt. 7:14).

The image of the journey as a symbol for spiritual growth has also been a favorite among contemporary writers other than Jung. C. S. Lewis used the image repeatedly in his books—for example, *The Pilgrim's Regress*, *The Great Divorce*, and in several of the Narnia tales. J. R. R. Tolkien, in his imaginative trilogy *The Lord of the Rings*, has caught something of the mysterious appeal of this image of the journey. His poem, "The Way leads ever on and on," is especially evocative. Richard Adams has his rabbits undertake a version of the Great Trek in *Watership Down*.

In my own experience of life as interpreted and guided by the peculiarly Christian experience, I have found that the image of a journey along a road is the one to which I return over and over. One may be lured away into side interests in the movement through life and get off the road. Salvation hymns and preaching refer to that experience as being "lost" and suggest that the way to be saved is through God. No one can say what "God" is; we have only intimations. The basic one seems to be that creative force—love.

It also seems to be the case that we need companions for the journey. A major teaching of psychotherapy is that there are times when we need to hold each other's hands as we move along the road of life. The biblical Ruth told her mother-in-law: "Where you go, I will go." This is a persistent refrain in songs about love. Road maps and guidebooks can be helpful (if we do not get lost in them), but there is great comfort in the warm, human sharing of problems and joys—even though, in the end, each one has to make the journey for him or herself. When friends of the spirit are not available in the flesh, we may find helpful the writings of those who have made the journey before us.

My teachers of the Way have been many and for all of them I am grateful. My contribution here is not so much to say something that has not been said before, but rather to share with my readers the road signs that I have found particularly helpful as I sought to make the journey.

The road signs in the chapters that follow are not the only ones; they are only a few of the ones that could be identified. None alone would adequately describe love. In the end love is known in a life lived. A definition of the early church's experience of love (still a felt-reality today) that has always appealed to me is that of the New Testament scholar John Knox, who called the church "the people who remember Jesus." It is a felt-reality of love lived out in Christian lives that speaks to us in the deepest sense. That was the point the medieval friar Francis of Assisi repeatedly emphasized in the founding of his new order. Incarnational Christianity finds its theme in the words of the fourth gospel: "And the Word became flesh and dwelt among us, full of grace and truth."

Most of the road signs identified in the following chapters apply to tasks and strengths to be devel-

oped in what Jung called the second half of life—
after one has developed what the psychologists call
a strong ego, a sense of one's own identity. They
are primarily for the mature adult who has found
a need for a new sense of meaning in life. They
suggest that an answer can be found through the
teachings of Jesus—that the way to wholeness is
a journey into love.

Spirituality is the term Christians have used to
describe their understanding of the stages of the
journey. The standard pattern in Christian spirituality has followed the three stages of the mystical
path or ascent: purgation, illumination, and union.
Purgation, as the term suggests, entails some cleans-
ing, some recognition of things that hamper one
in making the journey, and the replacement of those
with helpful attributes. Illumination refers to what
is learned along the way, insights that speed one
along the journey. The term "union" points to the
experience of the goal, whether the journey is understood as completed or simply nearing completion.
To some extent the chapters that follow could be
said to be contemporary road signs along the mystical way, the way that is a journey into love.

1

To Love Is to Grow

Speaking the truth in love, we are to grow up in every way into him who is the head, into Christ, from whom the whole body, joined and knit together by every joint with which it is supplied, when each part is working properly, makes bodily growth and upbuilds itself in love.

(Eph. 4:15–16)

The journey into love requires growth. Whether we call it spiritual growth or psychological development it is the same process. Just as the body has a pattern of growth, the nonphysical side of our being, whether called psyche or soul, requires some development. The development of consciousness is a process that begins with our birth. The child eventually learns to say "I" as it develops a sense of its own identity. Psychologists tell us that the development of a strong ego (the center of our awareness of ourselves as an individual) is a necessary attribute for psychic health. To what extent and how far we develop our consciousness or awareness depends on the circumstances life presents us with and our own exercise of choice.

Religious traditions throughout human history have described the goal of life and the kind of development that is to be sought. With the weakening of traditional perspectives for many in our pluralistic society, these answers have been largely missing. Philosopher Huston Smith writes: "Alexander Solzhenitsyn may go too far in seeing the contemporary West as 'spiritually exhausted,' but few seem to doubt a certain anemia."[1]

In our culture psychology has largely taken over the task of delineating the goal of human life and the stages of growth and development. Too often, however, the understanding of what *is* "the human" has been limited by the assumptions of the physical sciences. We focus on physical power, but we neglect the spiritual power that gives it meaning. As Huston Smith says: "Science in the form we have come to know it entered the seventeenth-century West as a new way of knowing, one that promised to augment our power and proceeded to deliver on that promise dramatically. The power it delivered has proved to be over nature only; it has not increased our power over ourselves (to become better people), or over our superiors (angels or God, let us say)."[2] Now ecologists are making us question this unlimited power trip over nature.

The goal a person seeks reflects, of course, the world-view of the particular religious tradition. That toward which the person seeks to move may differ widely depending upon the tradition—all the way from the fulfillment of being to the return to nonbeing. The Christian goal is described by Christopher Bryant: "An individual's spiritual development means growth toward a fuller union with God, through prayer, and a growing conformity to God's will in life."[3]

The longing for something "more," as William James called it, seems to be inate in the human psyche. Jung also told a group of pastors once that none of his patients in the second half of life had been really healed who did not recover a religious outlook on life. By that he meant a paying attention to something beyond the ego. Jung used the term "individuation" to describe the process of movement or growth toward wholeness. Jung considered individuation to be the psychological basis for the religious urge toward contact with the divine.

People long for transformation or a deeper understanding of themselves and their place in the world. Religious traditions have offered a path to follow with either a guide, or a set of guidelines, to aid them in making the journey. The road signs in this book suggest a way of growth in self-knowledge.

To find one's way or path requires self-knowledge, and much of the literature of Christian spirituality necessarily focuses on the encounter with one's self and with God. Augustine, the fifth-century bishop of Hippo in North Africa, was converted, he tells us in his *Confessions*, when he realized that God could be and had been experienced in his inmost being. It was possible, he concluded, because, as the Bible had said, we are made in God's image. Following Augustine's lead, the fourteenth-century English mystic Walter Hilton said, "A soul that desires to attain knowledge of spiritual things must first know itself."[4] Bonaventure, sometimes called the second founder of the Franciscan order, says that in the third stage of the journey one leaves behind the outer court and enters into one's inner self, there to strive to see God. St. Teresa of Avila in her *The Interior Castle* writes of a journey into a castle, into the inmost part of our being, there to find "the King," but not without difficulties on the way.[5]

The figure of the spiritual guide who accompanies one on the journey, helps one climb the ladder or follow the path is to be found in most religious traditions, whether the guide is called guru, master, rabbi, roshi, shaykh, pastoral counselor, or spiritual director. Most traditions have also recognized the legitimacy of an *inner guide*, but would expect that a relationship with the inner guide is seldom achieved without the aid of an outer guide. In the Hindu tradition, for example, it has been suggested that it is the inner guide who leads the disciple to the outer guru, and it is the outer guru who reveals the inner guide.

For Christianity, the inner guide is, of course, understood to be God's Holy Spirit. Yet a spiritual director or spiritual friend or pastoral counselor may be instrumental in helping one to discern the guidance of the Holy Spirit in one's life. The role of the spiritual director must never get between the directee and the Holy Spirit. In thinking about the role of the spiritual director I am reminded of the vow of Brother Roger who founded, shortly after World War II, the ecumenical monastery at Taizé, France. Brother Roger's vow was this: "to understand every person fully . . . instead of seeking to be understood."

The idea of spiritual direction is a very old one and of course not limited to the Western religious traditions. In the biblical tradition, the Wisdom literature of ancient Israel has some comments to the point. As rendered in the New Jerusalem Bible, Proverbs 3:5 says, for example: "Put not faith in your own perception," and again in Ecclesiastes 4:9–10: "Better two than one alone, since thus their work is really rewarding. If one should fall, the other helps him up; but what of the person with no one to help him up when he falls?" Proverbs 20:18 says: "Plans are matured by consultation; take wise advice when waging war." The idea of spiritual warfare encountered on the journey, and the need for all the help you can get with respect to it, is a pervasive theme in the New Testament as well.

In the language of the church, the Holy Spirit is "the Lord and Giver of Life." In the biblical story, it is God's Spirit that created the dry land and brought forth order and a new creation out of chaos. The Christian tradition teaches that this same life-creating Spirit still continues this same work in the lives of God's people.

Each person's spiritual journey is unique. The areas that need to be examined on the journey will differ from person to person and from time to time. The central concern in all spiritual growth is one's relationship with God. Anything that is blocking growth in this area is a matter for concern. Our relationship with God reaches into every part of our life, so that all kinds of issues become matters of concern on the journey: relational problems with family or at work, sexual concerns, compulsions, preoccupations, fears, emotional scars, angers and, of course, dreams or fantasies—all are grist for the mill in the matter of spiritual growth and development.

Prayer, meditation, contemplation—these are, and always have been, the royal road to lead one beyond the mundane world and into the presence of the divine. The spiritual masters have recommended a variety of exercises and practices to aid in achieving this goal. With regard to meditation, there have been two basic types. One tends to advocate an emptying technique, known as the *apophatic* approach. The other suggests an imaginal technique of meditation, known as the *kataphatic* approach. Both techniques can be found in the teachings of the spiritual masters of both East and West. Both the apophatic and kataphatic approaches can be seen as ways to move us out of the ordinary way we live in the world. They lead us on a journey either by directing us through images or by having us divest our mind of all images—an emptying by which we can reach a different experience. Techniques and exercises for both approaches have been developed for aiding one in making contact with the divine.

The Rule of St. Benedict has been a dominant pattern for monastic life. As a guide for an individual's development in prayer, the Rule insisted on *lectio divina*, or spiritual reading. From this experience, prayer was to come forth. The classic pattern was: first, *lectio* (reading), then *meditatio* (meditation), followed by *oratio* (prayer), and then *contemplatio* (contemplation). A contemporary description of a similar fourfold pattern comes from a Southern rural minister. The steps are these: I reads myself full; I thinks myself clear; I prays myself hot; I lets myself cool.

C. G. Jung, in addition to dream analysis, offered his students a method that he called "active imagination," by which the individual could carry on a dialogue with an image from the unconscious. In a similar way, the American depth psychologist Ira Progoff has developed an extensive set of techniques which he sets forth in his "Intensive Journal Workshops" by which the practitioner is guided in carrying on dialogues with material from the unconscious.

In his essay "The Stages of Life" Jung was perhaps the first to call attention to the "midlife crisis" as it has come to be called. He pointed out the difference in the "tasks" to be performed and the goal to be sought in the first half of life and the second half of life.[6] Jung believed there was a general movement in the psyche toward wholeness, toward a balance. The first half of life entails a moving into life and the building of an identity; the second half of life calls for the establishment of a relationship with something more, something beyond the individual ego. Failure to move on beyond the goals of the first half of life was a problem often encountered, Jung found.

For the mystics throughout the ages the stages of growth in the spiritual life and the goal toward which one moves have been understood as a journey toward oneness with God. The reality of the possibility of a direct encounter with God is, for many people, quite unsuspected. The difficulty of accepting this possibility is not peculiar to our contemporary Western culture, though perhaps it is more foreign to our century than to the high Middle Ages. (We really cannot be sure even of that, for the possible doubts and thoughts of the many people who could not read and write during the Middle Ages are generally not in the documents we have available to us. The basic human problems and concerns probably reach much further back into human history than we suspect.)

To love is to grow, to grow in our understanding of ourself and to grow in our understanding of the goal toward which life moves when the roadblocks are removed. Leaving behind what has been accomplished requires courage. Staying in the same place seems the safer choice, yet if there is no movement in our life a staleness sets in. Walled-in boredom seems to be the consequence of failure to undertake the journey.

To love is to grow. If C. G. Jung is right, as I suspect he is, undertaking the journey of growth in understanding is not only something that contributes to our own enlargement of life, but also contributes to society as a whole. Jung wrote: "In the last analysis, the essential thing is the life of the individual. This alone makes history, here alone do the great transformations first take place, and the whole future, the whole history of the world, ultimately spring as a gigantic summation from these hidden sources in individuals. In our most private and most subjective lives we are not only the passive witnesses of our age, and its sufferers, but also its makers."[7] That creative potential in each of us finds support in the biblical understanding that we are made in the image of God. There is a rabbinical saying: "Every human being is preceded by a legion of angels crying 'Make way for the image of God.'"[8]

If we do undertake the challenge, as Jung suggests, to contribute to society by undertaking our own journey of growth, it means making the journey into love. Love is not the easy attitude or feeling that our culture so often portrays or calls by that name. It is not an easy journey. To love is to make oneself vulnerable, but it is also the experience of wholeness and meaning in life.

2

To Love Is to Learn the Truth about Ourselves

He will come again to judge the living and the dead.

(from the Apostles' Creed)

Tell us, when will this be, and what will be the sign of your coming . . . ?

(Matt. 24:3)

"Here comes de judge" was a favorite laugh-appeal line on the television show "Laugh In" some years ago. The "coming of the judge" is an ancient motif in history. The expectation of *a day of judgment* is a feature of biblical religion from ancient Israel to the early Christian church. A number of different images are presented in the Bible. The early Christians who wrote the later books of the New Testament associated God's judgment with the return of their Lord which they expected momentarily. This came to be thought of as "a second coming." However, Jesus himself told a story about the "last judgment" which suggested that his "coming" was not just once or twice but repeatedly in all the events of life. More of this later.

None of us is quite comfortable in the thought of "facing the judge." Furthermore, with God's judgment there is the problem of its finality and no possibility of appeal. There is, however, an even more serious problem, and that is one of recognition: recognizing the Christ when he comes to us in judgment. Yet this too—even judgment itself— is a part of the experience of the journey into love.

When we think of facing the judge and judgment, I suspect most of us think about the criminal courts, and we tend to confuse the "judgment" with what is actually the "sentence." The sentence is the declaration of the amount of punishment, such as "five years in jail." Actually, the "judgment" is the *pronouncement of what is true*, such as "guilty of theft." In a civil-court case a "judgment" is always a declaration of whatever is found to be true in fact and applicable law: for example, "Brown owes Jones three thousand dollars." Some facts about *what is true* have been decided and declared. God's judgment, then, is "learning the truth about ourselves"—a declaration of what is true about each of us. Each time we see the truth about ourselves we are experiencing judgment. Yet the claim of Christianity is that this, too, is one of the road signs along the journey into love.

It is the Christ (God come to us) who reveals this to us, that is, lets us know what we are really like. But, even as Jesus said, we need to have "eyes to see" and "ears to hear" for discernment to take place. Let me try to illustrate the kind of thing I have in mind.

Suppose you had been trying for months to get your neighbor to go with you to the PTA or the civic club in your area. Finally, after trying all year and having quite a bit to say about "duty" and "responsibility," your neighbor does go with you. That night you happen to hear a talk about keeping the neighborhood neat and tidy and what can be done about that—just one of the many programs that year on civic responsibility. Then the next evening you are driving along, finishing a pack of chewing gum or a candy bar, and you chuck the wrapper out the window. Then you have to stop for a red light and the car behind you pulls up alongside you, and you happen to turn and look at the other driver. It is your neighbor, and you remember! He could not have failed to see you chuck the litter out on the street. There is nothing you can say. It's just the truth about you—you say one thing and do another! He knows it, but now you also know it about yourself. This is judgment—seeing the truth about ourselves. It seems to come home to us more clearly when others know as well.

Or, we may have told someone a lie for very good reasons. Most of us always have very good reasons for our lies. Then, through a chain of circumstances, that someone finds out. We stand revealed for what we are: a liar. We don't like the sound of that; it's too blunt. There is not much we can do to explain it; there never is after we are discovered, after the truth is out. Then our "reasons" seem inadequate. In this kind of event, God has come to us as our judge, if we can but know it.

God never forces an entrance, even in judgment. Such is the character of Love. In the event, whatever it is, we may be blind to the coming. We may not be able to accept the fact that "the truth is not in us." Our "very good reasons" may still cloud the issue for us. But the fact remains that even in coming to us in judgment, God comes to us in love. God comes into the world, St. John says, "not to condemn the world, but that the world through him might be saved." Or, to paraphrase St. Paul, "God loves us while we are still liars."

Sometimes it is only when our own inability and inadequacy are pointed up (only when we too cannot but learn the truth about ourselves) that we are able to see, to hear, and to discern. When we are able to do so, we find that God has come—not just to be our "judge" as we say in the Nicene Creed— but that the coming has also been "for us and for our salvation."

Depth psychologists have an interesting idea about one way to learn the truth about ourselves— by paying attention to our dreams. This new-old idea is very personal and direct. Jung's theory is that dreams are like snapshots of the psyche, revealing the "other side of the story"—that is, telling us what is in our unconscious. Furthermore, his theory says there is a compensatory relationship between consciousness and the unconscious. Thus, if we overemphasize something or omit something in our conscious life, the "other side" (or what is being omitted) is held up (as if for our attention) in our dreams. Both the Old and New Testaments, of course, are filled with stories of people paying attention to dreams, and most cultures have done so. Until the emergence of the depth psychologists modern Western culture, enamored with the possibilities in the development of reason, had ignored dreams as being of no value in our understanding of human beings. Now sleep researchers are finding that dreams are a necessary part of sleep time if the body is to awaken refreshed, and pastoral counselors are suggesting that this may be another way of learning the truth about ourselves.

Until we see the truth about ourselves, we cannot begin to be what we should be. But when we have been able to hear God's judgment, we find that we have been presented not only with a descriptive picture of the past and present, but also that a course of development for the future has been indicated. The way to go on the journey is being clarified by our seeing how far short of love we have fallen. We see the right road by seeing how far off the road we have gone—like a helpful native who points out the right highway when we are lost. When we see that self-knowledge is finding truth, not experiencing punishment, then we *know* that when God comes in judgment he comes in love.

I learned the meaning of God's judgment as "learning the truth about ourselves" for the first time some years ago when two things happened on the same day. The first thing happened when I was in a school bookstore talking to a friend when another student (let's call him Joe) came in. I did not particularly enjoy Joe's company. I did what I could to avoid a conversation. It was not easy to do. Almost from the beginning of my stay at that school it seemed that every activity threw us to-

gether: the same classes, the same small groups,
and the same adviser. I had tried, after a fashion,
to be nice to Joe, but he never seemed to understand
what I was saying and the effort seemed too much.
I knew he had some need of talking to someone
and that he had a problem with coming back to
school. He had told me about his family, but I never
remembered the names of his children.

I was still remembering the "near encounter"
with Joe when I got home, with my usual uneasy
feeling of discomfort. That evening I read a particular Bible passage, which was the second thing that
happened that day, leading up to my new experience
of judgment. It was the twenty-fifth chapter of Matthew in which Jesus tells a story about the "last
judgment"—how the sheep and the goats would be
separated on the right hand and the left.

> Then the King will say to those at his right hand,
> "Come, O blessed of my Father, inherit the kingdom
> prepared for you from the foundation of the world;
> for I was hungry and you gave me food, I was thirsty
> and you gave me drink, I was a stranger and you
> welcomed me, I was naked and you clothed me,
> I was sick and you visited me, I was in prison and
> you came to me." Then the righteous will answer
> him, "Lord, when did we see thee hungry and feed
> thee, or thirsty and give thee drink? And when did
> we see thee sick or in prison and visit thee?" And
> the King will answer them, "Truly, I say to you,
> as you did it to one of the least of these my brethren,
> you did it to me."

The parable goes on, and the King answers those
on the left who did it *not*. And that is where I

found myself standing, with the goats. Then, of course, I knew *who* it was I had left hungry for attention, thirsty for friendship, and as a stranger in the academic atmosphere of school. I had thought it was old Joe, but now I knew that it was Christ himself come to me. I was convicted; I saw what kind of person I was. I learned the truth about myself. Finding out "who we are" is a road sign to be followed if we are to make the journey into love.

Francis of Assisi is a good example of one who came to see the Christ in all the world around him. Early in his journey Francis learned one truth about himself when he recognized his horror at the sight of lepers. With Jesus' parable in mind he recognized who it was that was greeting him on the road— and, always quick to respond, he went to the leper and kissed him and tended to his needs. Discernment, for Francis, was not only learning something about himself, but also an opportunity for growth on his journey into love. God's judgment does not mean, as we have seen, the pain of punishment but rather the pain of insight. God's coming to us is in love, however, because we are left free to accept or reject (love does not coerce), and also we are offered the opportunity to grow and develop.

When the Christ comes to us in judgment, we know, as St. Paul would say, how far we "fall short of the glory of God." When the Christ comes to us, we know, as Isaiah did when he "saw the Lord sitting upon a throne, high and lifted up" and said: "Woe is me! For I am lost; for I am a man of unclean lips." So, also, with Peter, when he recognized who the Lord was, after the miraculous draft of fishes: "Depart from me, O Lord, for I am a sinful man!"

To love is to know God personally and not just theologically or philosophically. It is to know God, as the church is wont to say, "as our Lord and Savior," as the One in charge and the One who puts us back together. To love is to know God, to discern God in the midst of life. In this journey into love we are called to have that recognition at all times and in all places.

And God does come. It is not just "two comings"—the one remembered at Christmas and the "second coming" as the "end" of history. God comes to us over and over again as Jesus' story reminds us. The biblical view is that God *acts* in history and in the lives of people. God has a purpose and a plan, however open-ended that may be, which we may or may not conform to as we choose. God leaves us free, as love always does.

God comes into our lives; the problem is that of recognition. Did we smile at that tired and inexperienced clerk while we were doing our shopping? Did we recognize just who it was waiting at the stop sign on the cross street when we barged ahead from our stop sign with only a slight hesitation? How did we treat the person who works for us? What did we *say* about the person we work for?

If indeed it is, as I have suggested, that God comes to us in the everyday events of our journey through life, and we are thus enabled to see ourselves for what we are, then likewise in these same everyday events we are given opportunities to be what God has called us to be. The road has been marked off. One of the road signs reads: learn the truth about yourself.

3

To Love Is to Abandon Pride

For from within, out of the heart of man, come
evil thoughts . . . pride, foolishness.

(Mark 7:21–22)

Clothe yourselves, all of you, with humility toward
one another, for "God opposes the proud, but gives
grace to the humble."

(1 Pet. 5:5, quoting Prov. 3:34)

What is this humility of which Jesus, according
to Christian devotion, is an example? My dictionary
suggests two synonyms: lowliness and meekness.
If that is what the Christian life is about no wonder
a number of people are turned off by it! Are we
called to be what marriage counselors call a doormat
personality? Are we to provide the mat for the bul-
lies of this world to scrape their feet on? Surely
there must be a more positive aspect. If the meek
are to inherit the earth as Jesus said, meekness must
involve something more than being a doormat.

Humility and its synonyms are not qualities for
an attractive way of life, at least for English-speaking
people. (In my French Bible Jesus says: Blessed are
les débonnaires.) But humility is further defined
in my dictionary by saying what it is not. Humility
is the absence of pride and self-assertion. My wife
says that if learning what we are really like is what
God's loving judgment is (as suggested in the last
road sign), then humility is to go on living anyway,
even after we know.

In the twelfth century people were deeply concerned with the problem of love, carnal as well as
spiritual. The ideal of romantic love was portrayed
in the songs of the troubadors, and the nature of
God's love of us and of our love of God was the
focus of spirituality. It was for them, indeed, a journey into love. The dominant spiritual influence in
Europe at the time was the Cistercian monk Bernard
of Clairvaux. The soul's relationship to God was
the central theme Bernard developed in his numer-
ous sermons on the Song of Songs. In a manner
suggested by Augustine of Hippo, Bernard described
a psychological exploration of the soul, an inner pilgrimage by which the individual could experience
the love of God.[1] His starting point was the fact
of earthly love: the love of oneself and one's own
interests; then a higher form, the love of one's neighbor; and finally, the love of God.[2]

Bernard of Clairvaux taught that pride lessens a
person's worth. Humility, on the other hand, not
only recognizes one's need for God, but also demon-
strates one's capacity for God, thus revealing to us
what we are like.[3] We are needy and incomplete

without God, yes, but we also are creatures who can be in relation to God. He said humility thus means to know and acknowledge three things: first, to know our own limitations, our finiteness; second, to know that since everyone else shares the human condition we have no right to feel superior; and third, to know that the way to God is the way beyond our limitations.[4]

Richard of St. Victor, a contemporary of Bernard and prior of the Abbey of St. Victor in Paris, in his treatise on the four degrees of passionate love, described stages of spiritual development. He said the highest stage was not one of selfish withdrawal from the world, but rather one in which one humbled oneself and became the servant of others, as Jesus had done.[5] If humility is the absence of pride, then what are we to make of pride?

Pride is condemned in the New Testament and later became in the Christian tradition one of the "seven deadly sins." Perhaps by examining the nature of pride one can learn more about humility. There is a collection of teachings in the Sermon on the Mount that are commonly called the "Beatitudes" (Matt. 5:3–11), since in the King James translation they begin: "Blessed is . . ." The word which is there translated "blessed" means almost exactly what we mean by the word "happy" today. Since most people in this world desire above everything else to be happy, Jesus reveals the attitude of mind and the kind of conduct that lead to real and lasting happiness. J. B. Phillips has suggested that we may be able to see the contrast between Jesus' way and that of normal people—what might be called the

Way of Adam—if we first look at the "beatitudes of many ordinary people." That would run something like this, he says:

> Happy are the "pushers": for they get on in the world.
> Happy are the hard-boiled: for they never let life hurt them.
> Happy are they who complain: for they get their own way in the end.
> Happy are the blasé: for they never worry over their sins.
> Happy are the slave drivers: for they get results.
> Happy are the knowledgeable men of the world: for they know their way around.
> Happy are the troublemakers: for they make people take notice of them.[6]

Phillips's translation or paraphrase in modern language, quoted below, of what Jesus said is something quite different. Note that it is not so much a promise of a future reward in heaven as it is a "fact" about present life:

> Happy are the humble-minded,
>   for they already belong to the kingdom of heaven!
> Happy are those who know what sorrow means,
>   for they will be given courage and comfort!
> Happy are those who claim nothing,
>   for the whole earth will belong to them!
> Happy are those who are hungry and thirsty for goodness,
>   for they will be fully satisfied!
> Happy are the kindhearted,
>   for they will have kindness shown to them!

Happy are the pure in heart,
    for they will see God!
Happy are those who make peace,
    for they will be known as sons of God![7]

There is quite a contrast between the Way of
Adam and the Way of love. Notice what Phillips
does with the "meek." They are the ones who
"claim nothing." The proud are those who claim
everything for themselves, as the first list ("that
of many ordinary people") indicates. "Me first"
seems to be an inborn survival trait for humans,
as little children teach us. But part of what it means
to be human is to live with others, and as we grow
up we learn to overcome (or hide) our more obvious
selfishness. "Cultural evolution" is what one biolo-
gist has called this kind of development. Perhaps
this is also what the Buddha, the "one who woke
up," understood when he taught that craving must
be eliminated.

In Jungian psychology the sin of pride is known
as "inflation." Jung describes it as involving an extension of the personality beyond individual limits,
that is, as a state of being puffed up. It is an identifi-
cation by the ego with contents from the unconscious. In religious experience, it is appropriating
to the personal ego something belonging to God.
Jung writes about inflation:

This phenomenon, which results from the extension
of consciousness, is in no sense specific to analytical
treatment. It occurs whenever people are overpow-
ered by knowledge or by some new realization.
"Knowledge puffeth up," Paul writes to the Corin-

thians, for the new knowledge had turned the heads
of many, as indeed constantly happens. The inflation
has nothing to do with the kind of knowledge, but
simply and solely with the fact that any new knowledge can so seize hold of a weak head that he no
longer sees and hears anything else. He is hypno-
tized by it, and instantly believes he has solved the
riddle of the universe. But that is equivalent to al-
mighty self-conceit.[8]

Jungian analyst Edward Edinger warns that too
much humility as well as too much arrogance can
be a symptom of inflation.[9] In either case the ego
has overidentified with what Jung called the God
image within.

With respect to this road sign, Jungian psychology suggests an important caution. This road sign,
"abandon pride," applies to what Jung called "the
second half of life." It is for the mature adult who
has found in the story of Jesus "the way, the truth
and the life." It is not a task for adolescence or
for young people who are still finding their way
into life. Or, to use Jungian terms, the ego cannot
offer a sacrifice to something beyond itself until
the ego is strongly developed. One cannot sacrifice
that which one does not have. The term "pride"
is used, whether rightly or wrongly, to describe a
sense of accomplishment which is a helpful factor
in the building of ego—a task for the first half of
life. In this sense, this road sign is not directed
toward those with a weak ego development.

I once heard a new Christian comment on the
denigration of pride that is always found in Christian

teaching: how odd it was. He said, "I always thought it was a virtue." He went on to speculate: "If I didn't have pride, I wouldn't keep clean, or study, or strive at my job." He was speaking about the kind of tasks one quite appropriately needs to develop in the first half of life (and one does not abandon them with the coming of maturity). There is a difference, however, in the attitude one takes to those accomplishments. In other words, when we say we "are proud to be clean" (to use that example), it is all right if we simply mean we are glad and grateful for God's gifts which enable us to be clean; we are thankful for his gift of life and for the wherewithal that we enjoy, such as soap and running water, which we can use. It is all right to be "proud of doing a good job" if we are simply speaking of the joy of living which includes the joy of work, of doing what God has given us the talents to do well, and so to enjoy. The vice of pride lies in our attitude toward others. About this Christian scheme of morality, C. S. Lewis wrote:

There is one vice of which no man in the world is free; which every one in the world loathes when he sees it in someone else; of which hardly any people, except Christians, ever imagine that they are guilty themselves. I have heard people admit that they are badtempered, or that they can't keep their heads about girls or drink, or even that they are cowards. I don't think I ever heard anyone who was not a Christian accuse himself of this vice. And at the same time I have very seldom met anyone, who was not a Christian, who showed the slightest mercy to it in others. There is no fault which makes a man more unpopular, and no fault which we are more unconscious of in ourselves. And the more we have it ourselves, the more we dislike it in others.

The vice I am talking of is Pride or Self-Conceit. . . . .[10]

If Lewis is right, the way to find out about your pride is to consider how much you dislike it when other people ignore you, or perhaps are condescending in their approach. (It is because I want to be the center of attention that I am so annoyed at someone else being just that.)

In Jungian psychology this phenomenon is known as a shadow projection. What we do not recognize in ourselves or as a potentiality in ourselves we tend to see in others. It is not that the other person does not also have the particular characteristic; they have, as the Jungians say, a "hook" for the projection. Our own excessive emotional reaction to the other person, however, should provide us with the clue that a projection on our part is involved. To recognize a shadow projection in our irritation with someone else may provide us with a clue to the recognition of the vice of pride. As Bernard of Clairvaux said, humility comes when one really knows oneself.[11] This is not as easy, however, as it sounds. As G. K. Chesterton once said: "If I were the most humble man in all the world, I should be very proud!" C. S. Lewis wrote: "As long as you are proud you can't know God at all. A proud man is always looking down on things and people: and, of course, as long as you're looking down, you can't see something that's above you."[12]

The journey into love entails, for most of us, learning a new attitude toward our abilities—seeing them as gifts which we have been privileged to have the opportunity to develop. In line with this, one develops a new attitude toward others. The journey into love is always a matter of relationship: with ourselves, with others, and with God. I have found that the stance of thanksgiving is the fast lane on this journey into love. In giving thanks, we are not claiming too much for ourselves. When we give thanks to God we leave pride by the wayside. This sets us so free that the whole world is ours to enjoy. To love is to abandon pride.

4

To Love Is to Forgive

If anyone says, "I love God," and hates his brother, he is a liar; for he who does not love his brother whom he has seen, cannot love God whom he has not seen.

(1 John 4:20)

Forgive us our trespasses as we forgive those who trespass against us.

(from the Lord's Prayer)

To love is to forgive. Love is risky and it is costly for it entails forgiving. Forgiving, however, is the way to life and peace.

"Fair play" is dear to the heart of Americans. Fair play means you have a set of clear rules and everybody follows them and then no one gets stepped on. This is very helpful; I would not condemn it. The laws of ancient Israel sought to provide for fair play. The early American settlers were steeped in

43

the biblical sense of justice and fair play and sought
to express this in their new forms of government.

Under an ethic of fair play you would not do to
others what you did not want others to do to you.
That is a very good rule of fair play. Other rabbis
long before Jesus had taught that. There is really
nothing new with the golden rule. Jesus may have
turned it around and made it a positive "*do* unto
others," but Jesus' teaching on the demands of love
is more radical than that: love your enemies, forgive
those who despitefully use you. This is a further
development in the humility of "claiming nothing,"
the direction in which the last road sign pointed.

As the early members of the Christian community sought to understand their life-transforming
experience and the significance of Jesus in that experience, they described it in a number of ways:

—a new age dawning;

—the spirit of love had been "poured into
their hearts" even as the prophet Joel had
predicted;

—they were "in Christ" and he was in
them;

—Jesus was present with them in "the
breaking of bread";

—the ordering principle of the universe, the
logos, had been made flesh, that is, had entered into human life;

—the "ransom" had been paid.

Each of these interpretations found its way into the
New Testament. Clearly, for the early Christian, the
situation had changed. The basis for a new relationship had been revealed. There was no longer a separation from God. If sin was the state of being

separated from God, then what they had experienced was the "forgiveness of sin."

The apostle Paul wrote to the Christian community in Rome: "But God shows his love for us in that while we were yet sinners Christ died for us." In Paul's understanding the meaning of the cross is this: our separation from God has been overcome. We have been forgiven; the distance we created by our actions has been bridged. Paul described the experience in his letter to the Romans by saying, "we have access." The possibility of relationship has been restored. Furthermore, we have been forgiven that we might be able to forgive others and also forgive ourselves.

The author of the first letter of John wrote: "We love, because he first loved us. If anyone says, 'I love God,' and hates his brother, he is a liar; for he who does not love his brother whom he has seen, cannot love God whom he has not seen. And this commandment we have from him, that he who loves God should love his brother also." We have been forgiven that we might become forgivers.

To love is to forgive. Jesus had some very interesting things to say about forgiveness. In the Sermon on the Mount in the sixth chapter of Matthew, Jesus gives instructions about the practice of three spiritual disciplines which he assumes everyone follows: almsgiving, prayer, and fasting. He teaches about prayer with the exemplary prayer which we call the "Lord's Prayer," after which Jesus makes only one comment: "For if you forgive men their trespasses, your heavenly Father also will forgive you; but if you do not forgive men their trespasses, neither will your Father forgive your trespasses."

I am not forgiven until I forgive others! This is rough. This passage used to give me the idea that God was something like a bully, standing over me with a big stick, saying, "If you don't forgive him, I won't forgive you"—a most unpleasant picture, and more importantly not really consistent with what I thought I saw revealed about God in Jesus. Coercion is not a part of love. Later I came to see that my image or picture should be that of the "full pitcher." Unless I pour some out, there is no room for more of that living water. "Living water," as the Bible calls it, is running water; it is on the move—that is what keeps it from being stagnant. We have to give in order to receive; you have to pour from the pitcher to receive more into it. That is why Jesus said: "It is more blessed to give than to receive." He was not trying to talk us into putting more into the collection plate (even though that might take the brakes off on our journey into love), but rather to tell us a fact about the nature of love.

Forgiveness sounds like a lovely idea until we have something to forgive. Then we find out how costly it is. Then we begin to understand the meaning of the cross. Then our understanding turns to wonder at the words of Jesus on the cross: "Father forgive them." Forgiving others means that we are called upon to pay a price. A wife who repeatedly took back her faithless husband was asked once by her neighbor, who marveled at her behavior, how she could continue to forgive her husband only to have him be faithless again. What was it like? She replied: "It is just like dying."

We are able to forgive only as we are conscious of having been forgiven. This is what enables us to go out to another in forgiveness, to go out in love. "We love because he first loved us." It is true about forgiveness. We can forgive because we know we have been forgiven. Having learned and accepted the truth about ourselves and having experienced that in the context of God's love, we are enabled to move out with love to others. This gives us a rock to stand on from which we can reach out securely to others. The members of Alcoholics Anonymous can reach out to help others in a very demanding state because they remember being helped, and also they know that this giving of oneself is the way to health and wholeness for themselves.

The twelve-step program developed by Alcoholics Anonymous has been the most successful program in dealing with alcoholism. It has been adapted to many other life-problems, for example: Al-Anon (for family members of alcoholics), Adult Children of Alcoholics, Synanon, the Palmer Drug Abuse Program, and Overeaters Anonymous. The Twelve Steps of Alcoholics Anonymous are:

1. We admitted we were powerless over alcohol—that our lives had become unmanageable.
2. Came to believe that a Power greater than ourselves could restore us to sanity.
3. Made a decision to turn our will and our lives over to the care of God *as we understood Him.*
4. Made a searching and fearless moral inventory of ourselves.

5. Admitted to God, to ourselves, and to another human being, the exact nature of our wrongs.
6. Were entirely ready to have God remove all these defects of character.
7. Humbly asked Him to remove our shortcomings.
8. Made a list of all persons we had harmed, and became willing to make amends to them all.
9. Made direct amends to such people wherever possible, except when to do so would injure them or others.
10. Continued to take personal inventory and when we were wrong promptly admitted it.
11. Sought through prayer and meditation to improve our conscious contact with God *as we understood Him*, praying only for knowledge of His will for us and the power to carry that out.
12. Having had a spiritual awakening as the result of these steps, we tried to carry this message to alcoholics, and to practice these principles in all our affairs.*[1]

The twelve-step program is itself a description (with twelve road signs) of a journey of spiritual growth. The first step entails learning the truth about oneself and accepting it. Modern psychology has emphasized the necessity of self-knowledge which has always been the foundation stone of spirituality. Steps four through ten are related to the road sign here under consideration.

*The Twelve Steps are reprinted and adapted with permission of Alcoholics Anonymous World Services, Inc. "Permission to reprint and adapt the Twelve Steps does not mean that AA has reviewed or approved the content of this publication, nor that AA agrees with the views express herein. AA is a program of recovery from alcoholism. Use of the Twelve Steps in connection with programs and activities which are patterned after AA but which address other problems does not imply otherwise."—Alcoholics Anonymous World Services, Inc.

To love is to forgive, but how do you go about it? Over the years I have made a list of ways people have found helpful.

First, you might ask yourself: What is it about me that has been wronged? What is it I have to forgive? Or, what did the person do that really hurt *me*? Such an inquiry may lead us to conclude that it is really our inflation, our pride that is hurt— and that is part of *our* sin. As has been noted, pride is a wrong-way sign on the journey into love.

Secondly, we might get a clue from Jesus' "summary of the law." What does it mean "to love my neighbor as myself"? How do I love myself? It does not mean necessarily fondness or affection for myself—you can't just feel that by trying anyway— and I don't always like myself. It does not mean thinking the other person is good. Many people imagine forgiving enemies means making out that they are not such bad people after all. It is just the opposite. We are busy forgiving someone because they *have* done something wrong. For some, the Sunday school maxim may come to mind: "hate the sin; love the sinner." And that is it in a nutshell. If you have questioned how you can hate what a person did and not hate the person, C. S. Lewis says that there is *one* person for whom you have been doing that all your life—namely, yourself.

The third suggestion which "may bring it home to us," so to speak, is to forgive our "enemy" in the presence of another person, or by taking some other action that acts out our intention. One way of acting it out and in some way making it real for us might be to take it to Communion, to the Lord's Supper, as an offering of ourself to be broken. Some churches have specific provisions for this sac-

ramental method. In most, the minister in his coun-
seling role would be quite willing to be present to
a prayer of confession and to affirm the truth of
God's forgiveness. Many people have difficulty ever
accepting the truth that God loves them since God
must know what they are like. Very early most of
us are at least exposed to a wrong idea, and too
often it is drummed in: that we are loved only if
we are good. That is the worst thing we could be
taught, but it is so easy for even a Sunday-school
teacher to slip into—it is so helpful with the discipline. But if that were the truth, it would be more
"bad news." The "good news" of the New Testament is that we are loved—even at our worst. If
someone else, another person whom we can see,
knows the worst about us and still accepts us, then
we may be able to feel that we are acceptable or
that God loves us, which is to say the same thing.
This is the basis, of course, for the fifth step in
the Alcoholics Anonymous program.

Fourthly, one of the main problems of forgiving
is ever recognizing that we have anything to forgive,
to see that we are holding a resentment against another. Christians sometimes find this difficult because they are worried about "not judging the other
person," and so they will never let themselves say
that the other person is wrong (though they know
it deep inside). You can't begin to get rid of a resentment until you admit that the other person bears
some responsibility for your feeling. Modern psychology has taught us how easy it is for us to repress
resentments and yet how essential it is that we recognize them.

In getting rid of resentments, giving them to God,

you need to turn them loose completely. You have to turn your back on them and not pick them up again. One person told me about a friend who had owed her eight dollars for years. She couldn't get over her irritation, though she was ashamed to be so petty. Finally, she "gave" the eight dollars to God, promising that if the friend ever paid it back, she would give it away. Since it was now God's and not hers, she was able to lay down her resentment, seeing it more truly in perspective as a small and picky thing.

The last suggestion I would make about helping us to forgive is to accept forgiveness ourselves. This may seem like completing the circle: to forgive in order to be forgiven (or, in my image, pour out in order to receive) and then, to accept forgiveness in order to forgive (receive in order to pour out). It is. Each of us may enter the circle of truth at a different point, but to love is to forgive.

5

To Love Is to Listen

He who has ears to hear, let him hear.

(Matt. 11:15)

O God, by whom the meek are guided in judgment, and light rises up in darkness for the godly: Grant us, in all our doubts and uncertainties, the grace to ask what you would have us to do, that the Spirit of wisdom may save us from all false choices, and that in your light we may see light, and in your straight path may not stumble; through Jesus Christ our Lord. Amen.

(Book of Common Prayer, p. 832)

Listening is difficult. On the surface, it would seem there would be nothing to it. But it involves getting ourselves out of the way, and that isn't easy! There is a sacrifice of the ego in real listening. It involves giving up the right to control the direction of the conversation. The wishing-willing activity of the ego is put in abeyance. It involves waiting.

Perhaps I have learned more about myself in having to wait upon other people than in any other activity. It was not a pleasant thing to learn the full extent of my own impatience and self-centeredness. Waiting involves being open to who or what is coming. It is not a closed matter or one that you can determine. Much of the new mood in theological writing today focuses on the idea of waiting—of waiting upon God. Perhaps the message that needs to be heard (or that is waiting to be heard) by an impatient age is to wait.

There are different levels of listening. When we are listening to other people, it is one thing to hear the words that are said on the surface, and it may be quite another thing to hear what is "really" being said. A woman friend once told me about her experience with this kind of listening. As she was leaving for a meeting at her church, she heard her husband say to their preschool age daughter, "Don't ask Mommy now, dear, *nothing* must interfere with prayer group!" She heard the plea for more of her time by her husband, stayed home (without resentment— a necessary ingredient), and there was a new deepening and strengthening of their relationship. She acted out for him the love she felt for him which, of course, was greater than her feeling for the meeting. Listening is not just a passive activity. It involves making an offering of all that we are and have to give. I like to think of this as "listening with an inner ear."

There is a basic quality of "openness" about love from whatever side you view it. Listening involves this kind of openness. It is a matter of waiting and being willing to receive. It is a matter of giving oneself.

On an even deeper level, listening is also one kind of prayer. Of course there are other kinds, but surely listening is about half of what is involved in prayer. The great teachers of the path of spiritual development (the journey into love) sometimes speak of this kind of prayer (listening) as an aspect of the state of *contemplation*. Contemplation involves a withdrawal of attention from the sensible world and a turn inward. It is a creative activity, as the great creative artists—poets, painters, musicians—have found, and it requires a kind of submission of the will.

Teresa of Avila, the great spiritual teacher of the sixteenth century (recognized by the Roman Catholic church as a "doctor," that is, "teacher" of the church) described four degrees of prayer.[1] The first one, for beginners, she compared to the labor involved in drawing water up from a deep well. The labor involved, however, is well worth the effort. When one moves to the second degree of prayer, less labor is involved. Teresa compares it to having a device with a pulley which makes watering the garden easier. In this stage, one has learned to still the senses; the distractions are less intrusive. The third stage she compares to being able to water the garden by irrigation from a nearby spring or stream. Some effort is still required, however, in directing the water into the proper channel. In the fourth stage, it is as if the watering of the garden is simply provided by God's rain. The closer we approach God in our attentiveness, the easier it becomes, as God comes to meet us and help us. It takes, however, as Teresa warns, higher degrees of prayer.

As individuals persevere in their journey into love the Holy Spirit brings about a transformation of their approach to life. Prayer becomes simpler, as Teresa suggested, and they find God's leading easier to discern and follow. Furthermore, in listening for guidance and following through, they find themselves freer, more wholehearted, more truly themselves than ever before.

To love is to listen. On the journey into love, action is called for, but first we have to listen to know what that action is. There should be "receiving" before we move out. Bernard of Clairvaux has a warning: "It is the property of the everlasting and just law of God that he who is not willing to be ruled gently is ruled painfully by himself, and he who is not willing of his own free will to take up the gentle yoke and light burden of love will bear against his will the insupportable burden of his own will."[2] The idea here is to listen before we leap.

To love is to listen. This means, first of all, to learn God's will for us. The prayer for guidance is typified by Jesus' prayer in Gethsemane in which he sought to know the Father's will. He hoped that will was not what he dreaded, but he promised to follow whatever it was. It involved waiting, which his disciples were not able to do without going to sleep.

The need for listening "with an inner ear" has been rediscovered in our day outside the context of biblical religion in depth psychology. For example, Jung built a place where he could go apart to be quiet and listen. He thought of it as listening to the unconscious. The "tower" at Bollingen on the shores of the upper lake at Zurich became not only his "place" personally, but also a symbol for him and his students of this necessary aspect of life—listening. In addition to the personal unconscious, Jung distinguished a "collective unconscious"—that mysterious something shared with all humanity, which could influence a life and provide guidance. Jung's personal discovery of this factor in the psyche, that is, the possibility of an encounter with something beyond the material in the personal unconscious, had an effect on his life comparable to that of Augustine, whose discovery of this "reality" changed his life and led to his conversion to Christianity. Late in life, when questioned about whether he believed in God, Jung replied, "I don't need to believe, I know."[3] Jung, as a psychologist, tried to avoid making statements about the theologians' "God," who was the unknown and unknowable. But he did make a study of our "messages" from the unknown, or the unconscious, as he would call it.

Jung had another way of speaking about this kind of listening. He called it discovering one's own personal myth. A myth, as Jung uses the term, is a story that conveys meaning and truth. To discover one's personal myth is to learn one's identity in the deepest sense. He wrote on the opening page of his posthumously published autobiography, "What we are to inward vision, and what man appears to be *sub specie aeternitatis*, can only be expressed by way of myth. Myth is more individual and expresses life more precisely than does science."[4] To learn one's myth, to do this kind of listening, is to respond to a "call." The real meaning of *vocation* is to be called. For Jung, learning one's myth is the way to wholeness; it is the goal of life. In religious language, this means learning what God has made one to be. Jung describes the experience of such a vocational call: "It is a very different thing when the psyche, as an objective fact, hard as granite and heavy as lead, confronts a man as an inner experience and addresses him in an audible voice, saying, 'This is what will and must be.'" Then, Jung said, one feels oneself called.[5] Jesus, however, suggested that not everyone had "ears to hear." One must listen. The religious person hears the call as coming from God, and the only faithful response then is to keep his commandment. "I can do no other," Christians have said down through the years. Once we move into the modality of listening, we may find it to be as Bernard of Clairvaux described it: "There is no need to make an effort to hear this voice. The difficulty is to shut your ears to it. The voice speaks up; it makes itself heard; it does not cease to knock on everyone's door."[6]

The journey into love does not mean only giving, such as listening, though it certainly includes that. It also means being loved by God and knowing it. The finding of one's own myth, one's own proper "vocation," is the surest route to joyful knowledge of God's love. As St. Gregory said, "Love itself is knowledge: the more one loves, the more one knows."[7]

There is a story in the New Testament about this kind of listening and *obedience* that has a particularly human ring to me. It is the story of the Annunciation, of an angel coming to Mary to tell her of bearing Jesus. St. Luke tells us (1:26–47) that Mary

was troubled by the angel's greeting: "Hail, O fa-
vored one, the Lord is with you! Blessed are you
among women!" If we let Mary be human, we can
imagine how she must have felt. Did she wonder
if she was "making it up"? Even after the angel
reassures her and gives her his message, she asks,
"How can this be?" And she is told about her cousin
Elizabeth, who in her old age is also to have a son.
With God, nothing is impossible, the angel assures
her. And so Mary consented, in obedience, "Let it
be to me according to your word." But then the
angel departs. Perhaps Mary wondered again if the
whole thing were real. Had she indeed had a vision
or was it the product of her own imagination? How
often this happens to us. We are forced to choose
how to respond to our listening. Mary doesn't sit
around and do nothing! A woman friend of mine
once suggested that Mary set out on a walking journey (surely not too pleasant in the early stages of
pregnancy) to check on her guidance, to see if Elizabeth was going to have a baby. Her sign had been
the conception by Elizabeth, and only after Elizabeth speaks out her own guidance is Mary's joy
so full that she bursts forth with the beautiful words
of the Magnificat: "My soul magnifies the Lord,
and my spirit rejoices in God, my Savior."

To love is to listen. But how? To listen to God,
to the inner voice, requires first the decision to do
so and then a following through. Most people have
found a regular time, a "quiet time" to be the most
helpful way. Setting aside a particular time and perhaps even a particular place helps to focus our
"openness." Most of the "saints" down through the
centuries have witnessed to this experience. It needs

to be done daily. In whatever way we arrange it, there should be some time of becoming inwardly still, knowing that God is, and waiting on him. "Speak Lord, for your servant listens"—instead of what too many of our prayers are: "Listen, Lord, for your servant speaks."

I think it is wise to wait with pencil and paper. So many times, it seems, the thoughts that spring to mind strike us as so insignificant that we try to dismiss them. If we write down these thoughts, however, we may find that we have a list of things that need attention. Furthermore, even if our list does not include items that need doing, simply writing them down enables us to stop thinking about them and may open the door to our being receptive to "hearing" something else. One person trying to keep her first quiet time with pencil and paper beside her ended her spiritual exercise with only "cat food and toilet paper" on her list. Yet frivolous as this seems, they were needed items for her household and provided a shopping list.

Not all of the guidance is this simple, even if it seems to be. In fact, the results are often surprising. If you make a telephone call to someone whose name has come to you, you frequently hear them say, after chatting awhile, something like this: "Oh, it's good to talk to you; I was really low this morning and I feel so much better." Your obedience to the "call" which seemed so trivial is thus more than you thought. Listening and obeying become a way of loving. Discipline is the key.

In this century depth psychology has taught us a new way to listen and that is to listen to our dreams, as I mentioned earlier. To do this, discipline has to come to the fore. If we do not record the dreams as soon as we wake, they slip away and are forgotten. Dreams give us a picture, one might say, of just how it is with our inner being. They can call to our attention aspects of our perspectives on life that we have ignored or viewed from a skewed vantage point. Dreams do not tell us what to do; they simply give us information, and it is up to us to decide what action, if any, we wish to take. In the Bible we have recorded mostly the interpretation or understanding that was gleaned from dreams and the action that was decided upon as a consequence. Unlike our contemporary world, the world of the Bible had no difficulty in accepting the reality of the spiritual world— what psychology today calls psychic reality. Dreams and visions were an obvious source for guidance.

To love is to listen.

6

To Love Is to Offer

. . . the prayer of faith will save the sick.

(James 5:15)

This road sign on the journey into love involves a quite different kind of prayer than simply listening. This sign says: OFFER. To offer is to give of ourselves to God and to give of ourselves to other people, according to God's purposes for us. Romano Guardini has written: "The prayer that God's will be done therefore does not mean that the inevitable should be fulfilled and that we are prepared to resign ourselves to it. The will of God is not a fate which has to be endured, but a holy and meaningful act which ushers in a new creation. The demand is that the work should be fulfilled in the way which helps that creation most."[1] This road sign calls for a kind of prayer that involves action. One form of active prayer is what the letter of James in the New Testament calls "the prayer of faith" (5:15).

Most of us understand "faith" to be something

more than "believing the unbelievable"—I've never been able to see how anyone could really do that. As St. Augustine said in his essay on the Trinity: faith is not that which is believed, but that by which it is believed.[2] Faith in the New Testament means trust, dependence upon, reliance upon, confidence in—and it is all of these. The kind of action called for in this road sign, "to love is to offer," involves all these attributes of faith. It is an offering of myself for God's purposes.

We can give of ourselves in a number of ways. In addition to giving of our money, we can, for example, visit the sick, take food or provide transportation for those in need. Most cities and communities, as well as churches, have places that need and welcome volunteers for this kind of activity. This road sign, however, points to a different kind of offering—the offering we make, or can make, in prayer.

In the Sermon on the Mount Jesus gave advice on how to live creatively. He spoke of three spiritual disciplines that he assumed everyone was practicing. He said *when* you give alms, *when* you pray, *when* you fast do it this way and not that way. He assumed a disciplined spiritual life which included prayer. Discipline is not, however, easy. It always includes giving up something of ourselves. Giving alms is giving a large part of our lives: the time we spend earning a living. Fasting involves giving up a part of ourselves that is very close to us: our appetites. What do we give up in the "middle" discipline?

What I think we have to offer in prayer is our imagination, our creative imagination. This must be, it seems to me, the heart of what the Bible calls the "prayer of faith." We are made in God's image, one of the old biblical stories says. What we share with God is not our physical makeup, obviously. Perhaps it is our imagination, our ability to make images in our thoughts. Imagination is the ability to "see" something done and accomplished and to "see" what it would be like even before it is done. All creative activity begins this way. Inventors have to imagine before they can make. Artists "see" before they paint. Even the Creator "moved upon the face of the waters" before beginning the acts of creation.

C. G. Jung had a technique for consulting the unconscious which he called *active imagination*.[3] He distinguished this process from mere passive fantasy, which can be destructive of time, accomplishment, and personality. Active imagination is not the dreaming adolescent or Walter Mitty, the fantasy hero. Instead, one offers oneself to the flow of images from the unconscious, yet retains a conscious point of view. There is a specific focus—perhaps a dream figure or a puzzling question to be solved in daily life or an emotion to be understood. The solution from the unconscious remains subject to the logic of the conscious mind, yet unless the conscious mind has opened itself to the unconscious images by an offering of its "sovereignty," the images would not be available as a part of the raw material of the solution.

Ira Progoff, with his Intensive Journal Workshops and Dialogue House publications, has developed helpful techniques for carrying out the dialogue between consciousness and the unconscious.[4] In a

sense his dialogue techniques are an elaboration of
Jung's concept of active imagination, but with more
specific directions on how to do it, on how to focus
one's attention.

I think the prayer of faith requires a similar offering of one's attention. If what we have to offer in
prayer is our creative imagination, that is, the ability
to make pictures and see the thing done, with confidence and expectancy, then we cannot make the
offering with confidence and expectancy unless we
first have listened. Otherwise, we would not know
what to picture in the offering of our imagination.
However, in some cases, if we have been able to
"hear" the gospel, the good news of God's love of
us and all creation, then we may already be confi-
dent of God's purposes with respect to some things.
We already know that God is at least as good as
our notion of what is good, but for some things
we do not know what is good, and so we seek guidance first; we listen.

Bishop Browning, the presiding bishop of the Epis-
copal church, has remarked about prayers for healing: "Healing teaches us that there is a person there.
Not just a force. Not just a principle. There is a
person out there who loves us and wants the best
for us. I don't think I really knew that before I experienced that healing. We don't need to ask 'What is
God's will concerning healing? . . . God's will is
life in fullest abundance. It's health. It's not now,
and never has been, and never will be sickness and
death."[5]

One of the difficulties with this prayer of faith
for many people is that it seems too much like asking Santa Claus for a favor. We don't want to be

childish, even if Jesus did suggest that we must be childlike in our approach to the Father. Jesus himself certainly included a request for "daily bread" in his sample prayer.

This matter of particularity has always been a part of the Christian message and Christian faith. That God acted at a particular time and a particular place found its way even into the ancient Creed of the church: "suffered under Pontius Pilate." To most philosophers and some theologians this particularity—of God's action in history, in a *particular* place and a *particular* time—has always been, and still is, the "embarrassing" thing about Christianity. It is, for them, as St. Paul said, the "scandal" of Christianity.

Many good people, I suspect, feel it is not appropriate to ask for specific material things in prayer. However, if that is where our energy is focused, we are simply shutting God out of that area of our life. We are simply refusing to let God into the picture.

The objections to prayers for material things are probably based on one or more mistaken ideas. First, that God cannot or will not do anything about the way the world is. Many people feel this way but simply do not let it come to the surface of their thinking or follow through on the implications. In contemporary literature, such an idea is put in ultimate terms; God is either dead or absent, but certainly not the *living* God portrayed in the Bible. Process theology, however, says God is actively engaged with creation and seeks to lure us into contributing, as co-creators, to the fulfillment of God's purposes.

Secondly, the reluctance to pray about material concerns may stem from the idea that God is interested only in the spiritual, not the material. This is a nonbiblical approach that denies God's work in creation. The idea finds its way into Christianity at times in "flight-from-the-body" approaches. In the ancient world there was a widespread notion that the body was simply the prison house of the soul. This was not the position in the Jewish world. The biblical story of creation, whatever else it may not tell us, at least tells us this. The refrain in the Genesis story of creation keeps on being repeated: God looked at it . . . and it was good. Christianity is, as Archbishop William Temple said, "a materialistic religion." God is concerned with the physical and material as well as the spiritual. Christianity's approach is world-affirming.

The biblical picture presents humanity as responsible. We are assured of God's steadfast love, and in turn we are called to walk the road of that love ourselves. We have a part to play in the fulfillment of God's purposes, which is to say that our lives have meaning. To be loved and know it, the psychologists tell us, is to be *enabled* to love. To love is to offer something of ourselves in response to the love we have known.

One thing we can offer the great Creator of life is our own creativity by becoming a part of the continuing creation of life. This kind of approach helps me to understand the biblical injunctions for petitionary and intercessory prayers—"asking" prayers. Jesus is reported to have taught, "Ask, and it will be given you; seek, and you will find; knock, and it will be opened to you. For everyone who asks receives, and he who seeks finds, and to him who knocks it will be opened."

In petitionary and intercessory prayer, surely we are not telling God something that is not known. Rather, in our words and thoughts we are offering our creative energy for the accomplishment of God's purposes, just as we can offer our hands, our feet, our money. Our creative imagination is perhaps the distinguishing thing about people. All that humanity has made, vast as it now is, started out in human imagination. So in our prayers of asking we use our creative imagination to see (in our mind's eye) God's purposes being effected in whatever way we can best understand that. God's response will, no doubt, be according to God's purposes, but it seems that we can make a contribution.

To love is to listen, and to love is to offer. Both these road signs are suggested, I think, in one of the old prayers of the church: "O Lord, from whom all good things do come; Grant to us your humble servants, that by your holy inspiration we may think those things that are good, and by your merciful guiding may perform the same." Both ideas are here: the need for guidance, the listening, and the prayer that we may, by "holy inspiration," use our creative imagination, or "think those things that are good."

After enjoining his listeners to ask, seek, knock, Jesus continued: "Or, what man of you, if his son asks him for a loaf, will give him a stone? Or if he asks for a fish, will give him a serpent? If you then, who are evil, know how to give good gifts to your children, how much more will your Father who is in heaven give good things to those who ask him?" (Matt. 7:7–11). It seems too good to be true, doesn't it? But don't knock it unless you've tried it. For two thousand years there have been people who did try it and found that it was true.

Even if we are not sure what God's purposes are, the point is to go ahead and pray about it anyway, to make the offering. As Jesus said, go ahead and ask, seek, knock. In prayer, we at least let God *in* on the situation. God waits to be invited; we are all quite free as to whether we extend the invitation. Note that this is a place for honesty. The One whom we are addressing is the One "unto whom all hearts are open, all desires known and from whom no secrets are hid." So in prayer we are not to try to hide what we really feel or want. If we are simply honest about it and then seek to pray for the accomplishment of God's purposes, then God can come in to increase our trust. And, being invited in, God may cleanse our desire so that it is changed or taken away. Or we may find (happy surprise!) that God's purposes coincide with our desires. Either way, our needs are met and, as Jesus said, "our joy may be full."

We do well to remember the visions of the fourteenth-century English mystic Julian of Norwich who, in her thirty-first year, as she tells us, when she was near death, received a series of visions or "showings" as she called them. One of the most striking passages reads as follows: "And so our Lord answered to all the questions and doubts which I could raise, saying most comfortingly: 'I may make all things well, and I can make all things well, and I shall make all things well, and I will make all things well; and you will see yourself that every kind of thing will be well.'"[6]

Many of us may not be able to stir up the confidence of Julian of Norwich when we offer our "prayer of faith." However, who knows just how the imagination works? When we make the offering we have at least opened the door for communication and then we can leave it in God's hands.

To love is to offer.

7

To Love Is to Accept

This is my commandment, that you love one another as I have loved you.

(John 15:12)

To make the journey into love is to experience the "newness of life" that Easter symbolizes. Easter and resurrection, however, are preceded by the cross of Good Friday. To love is to accept the mystery of the cross. Surely the first thing that confronts you about Christianity is the cross, from the cross on church buildings and in stained glass windows to handsomely wrought jewelry. Anyone coming in from an alien culture would surely ask, "Why?" and perhaps, "What is it that happened?"

The cross is a mystery, the understanding of which, I am sure, deepens for the Christian throughout life. That is the way with a symbol. It is like going down a corridor in which doors keep opening as you come to them. The cross, in Christian theology, has to do with our at-one-ment with God. No one theory of how this takes place has ever been given universal approval by the church. The mystery remains and so, for many, does the truth of the experience, despite our tendency to doubt the reality of that which we cannot explain.

What is it that happened? The Christian story says that God so loved the world that in Jesus the divine became one with the human. What happens when love enters into a sinful (that is, an estranged, "fallen") world? Sin always crucifies love. Sin is separation; love is relationship. For God to enter into humanity, for Jesus, the Cross meant denial of himself, of his egocentered will, and obedience to the Father's will: namely that he *be* love.

The cross was a voluntary offering. This is not always clear when we think about what the cross means to us. The synoptic gospels have a number of accounts of Jesus advising us "to take up our cross" and follow him. Thus, in the sixteenth chapter of Matthew: "Then Jesus told his disciples, 'If any man would come after me, let him deny himself and take up his cross and follow me. For whoever would save his life will lose it, and whoever loses his life for my sake will find it.'" The "deny himself" does not refer simply to "doing without" things; it is more complex than that. It means to make a voluntary commitment, an offering of oneself to be in relationship with God's call. The cross does involve pain; it is a death of the egocentered will and the acceptance of a path that involves relationship with God. It is, however, an offering we have chosen to make, as the earlier road signs have indicated.

Thus, "taking up *our* cross," is not a calamity

that occurs. A grief or sorrow is not a cross in this sense, even if it is a heavy burden. It is not something we "take up"—we have no choice. Our migraine headaches cannot be "our cross" in this sense, for we do not voluntarily choose them. If we did, we would not take aspirin. It is not our shortcomings of temperament and dispositions, our uncontrolled anger, our undue sensitiveness or impatience. These are things we have to live with, to learn to control. The call of the Christian life, however, involves a more complete commitment of ourselves than simply bearing the burden life presents. "Taking up our cross" is not "enduring stoically" what happens to us. This may be a virtue, but Christianity is more than the modern Stoicism into which it is sometimes distorted. The cross was for Jesus a deliberate choice of giving his life, in obedience to the Father's will, rather than human will. The cross which he bids us take up is a self-giving. To choose to follow the way of the cross appears, before we do it, to be a matter of giving up our life. Looking back, however, after passing through the gate, having made the choice, it seems as though we have really found our true self. Good Friday is followed by Easter.

Indeed, it seems that we are made for this kind of self-giving. We all long to be committed to a cause, a thing, or a person. This is the way we seem to function. Yet there are immense difficulties involved. Some of us have difficulty ever giving of ourselves at all. Others give, give, give, but with the wrong orientation—a kind of giving that drains a person. The giving may be to a business, a wife, or a child, but it may not be what is called for.

This kind of "overgiving" (that is, where ego chooses the "gift" that is given) drains a person, not to mention the effects on the recipient. It becomes simply a loss of life. The cross involves a self-giving of ourselves to God and then, as we are led, to others. Strangely enough, in this kind of self-giving (understood as a giving to God), we find ourselves to be more truly ourselves than ever before. We are not drained but filled. It is as if we had been reborn and found our true identity.

In this resurrection life one "abides in love," as Jesus called it. We have the confidence to make the journey into love, to accept ourselves and to accept God's love because of two presuppositions well established in the New Testament. The first one is simply that God is good. If you don't know this, then you are missing a lot in the Christian faith. If your religious perspective is limited to a moralistic viewpoint, then you haven't heard the "good news" the early Christians were shouting about. Rather, God must be "bad news," as in fact is the case for so many. If God is experienced as demand-for-perfection without also being experienced as complete acceptance, that *is* bad news.

When we think of God as personal, we think of God as loving, just, true, patient, and so on. When we enlarge our picture and think of God as the symbol for the ultimate meaning of the universe, that which underlies all that is, then we are saying that ultimate meaning also is good—that despite the evil, the muck, and the pain that comes to us in this world, there is, ultimately, goodness. Christianity does not deny the existence of evil but affirms that ultimately it will be overcome.

The second presupposition follows from the first: namely, that God's creation is good. Over and over, in the first chapter in the Bible, comes the refrain after an act of creation, "And God saw that it was good." Basically, the Bible is not to be read for history, although there is a surprising amount of historical material there. But that is not the main point. The stories in the Bible were told and then read for thousands of years. That surely indicates that the stories resonated with the deepest experience of people over the centuries. The Bible continued to be read because it encompassed existential truths: truths about "felt-realities," about the the way life is when you live it.

The Jewish and Christian traditions are world-affirming. We are not to "escape" this world by killing all desire. Rather than kill desire, we are to have our desire poured forth into the right mold for its adequate fulfillment. C. S. Lewis has expressed the Biblical understanding of this in beautiful imagery in *The Great Divorce*, where the "lizard" of lust, when rightly redirected—though in a process that required some pain—became the beautiful white stallion Desire, upon which the pilgrim could ride forth on the journey toward love. Every human instinct has its potential for good. Jung's concept of the shadow also illustrates this point, with its understanding that becoming aware of the shadow and consciously integrating some aspect of it into our life adds a dimension of strength and energy previously unavailable.

At times in its history, the church has forgotten this presupposition about the goodness of God's creation. At times it has succumbed to what might

be called a counterculture perspective that separates
body and spirit. One can see this, in both Protestant
and Catholic forms, in the difficulties in dealing
with sex, celibacy, and material goods. Body and
spirit cannot appropriately be separated; both are
what it means to be human. Both are part of God's
good creation.

So what follows from these two presuppositions:
that God is good and that God's creation is good?
First, as part of God's good creation we can assume
that we, being a part of it, are acceptable. No matter
how experience may have fashioned us, the potential
for good is there. We can make the journey into
love without losing our personal identity. Secondly,
we can assume that God did not make a mistake
with me—nor did God make a mistake in the creation of my wife, or my roommate, or my office
"friend," or my child, and so on. It really is the
"good news." That is why it sells so well. The book
title of a long-time best seller says what everyone
wants to hear: *I'm OK, You're OK*.

This is not always easy to remember. The trouble
is that *people are* different. A number of psychologists have attempted to catalog the typical ways in
which people are different. This can help us to begin
to understand what it is like, as the American Indi-
ans said, to stand in another person's moccasins.
C. G. Jung's explorations in typology have been the
most helpful to me. Jung's system has been made
more available to people generally through the
Myers Briggs Type Indicator developed by two American women.[1] The system involves two attitude
types, extravert and introvert, and the recognition

of four functions: sensing, thinking, feeling, and intuition. The wonderful thing about this typology is that in this understanding there is no "wrong" way to be, nor is one type "better" than another. Each of them may be used well or used poorly. Each type is an acceptable way of being.

Another rather elaborate system developed in the Sufi tradition is that of the Enneagram. This system, too, affirms the acceptability of each type and points out strengths and weaknesses and areas for growth. Each one of these systems can show us this truth that is so hard to believe. No one system can contain all the miracle of variety, but any one system can help us believe the differences enough to be honestly accepting. To love is to accept—to accept the fact that we are different. I don't have to be like other people, and other people don't have to be like me.

God seems to have thrown away the pattern with each individual. We even see this love of variety, this superabundance of creative energy in the rest of nature. Even the snowflakes are all different, we are told, as well as leaves off the same tree. So even though we are different, it is no mistake. To love one another is to accept one another, just the way we are—before we change. To love is to accept one another without waiting for the other person to correct his or her "faults."

The kinds of differences I especially have in mind are sometimes subtle and not always recognized as truly differences. That is when it is hard to accept. When we think (as my wife used to say she thought about me): "He's just being that way on purpose, in order to win or just to be mean," we need to take a second look. He may be; but it is also possible that he looks at the world differently. Henry David Thoreau understood this when he wrote: "If a man does not keep pace with his companions, perhaps it is because he hears a different drummer. Let him step to the music which he hears, however measured or far away."

Some differences in people can be seen in the quickness of reactions and the strength of reactions. For example, you tell your friend about something of great interest to you and about which you are quite excited, and he doesn't react. In all likelihood, he is not doing that on purpose, but he is simply being himself. He doesn't react quickly and with enthusiasm . . . until later. Then, for you, it may be too late; a resentment has already come between you.

One couple described a difference between their two teenagers. They had one who could hear only if you shouted at him, both literally and figuratively. The other one could *not* hear if you did shout. Or another friend says that with his two children he has to be quite different in order to do the loving, caring thing. If one comes home with a *C*, he has to say, "What's a *C*!" and make light of it, or the child would be devastated and unable to work. With the other child, on the other hand, he had to scream, "A *C*—you can do better than that!" in order for him to be encouraged to work at all.

Another kind of difference appears in this situation. One person likes to have things settled, while the friend or partner prefers "to keep the options open" and not make a decision. That spells trouble, whether in the office or at home.

To love is to accept ourselves and to accept other people, just as they are. This is the way God accepts us, as one of the old hymns says, "just as I am . . . ."

You might say God has made us from different molds, and it is all right. We may not be fully responding to the potentialities that have been given us and we may need to change and cut out some things and add some things, but the basic way we are, our basic mold, is acceptable even though we may not have yet fulfilled our potentialities. God accepts us and loves us, just as we are, before we have even responded to what help and love can do with us.

To love is also to accept a free gift. This is another aspect of the acceptance that is involved in the journey into love. We don't earn love; it is always a free gift. If it isn't, it's not love but something else. That we are not dependent upon ourselves, that God loves us without our being able to "keep the law," is what so thrilled the apostle Paul. It is indeed good news that we are not dependent upon our own efforts. Rather, the Christian story is: that God has acted for us, that we are loved that much. This is the rock from which we can move out to others: we are loved, and so we can love. One of the New Testament writers put it quite bluntly long ago: "We love because he first loved us" (1 John 4:19).

It is a humbling fact—this matter of accepting a free gift. Our pride is humiliated in the acceptance of this "handout" at the hands of God. None of us especially likes what we call "charity." We don't want to accept a handout—from anybody, not even God. This is the great stumbling block of the gospel: that the free handout is the only way to life, that we cannot earn our way in the life of love. We cannot make the journey into love and offer anything, except our love, in response to love. To love is to experience acceptance—and to accept.

8

To Love Is to Hope

No, in all these things we are more than conquerors
through him who loved us. For I am sure that neither
death, nor life, nor angels, nor principalities, nor
things present, nor things to come, nor powers, nor
height, nor depth, nor anything else in all creation,
will be able to separate us from the love of God
in Christ Jesus our Lord.

(Rom. 8:37–39)

To love is to hope. To many people hope seems
childish, with no basis, but merely a wishing
upon a star. The phenomenon of hope, however, is
grounded in existential experience. The Christian
philosopher Gabriel Marcel pointed out in his *Homo
Viator* that hope about the future springs from a
present experience or the memory of a past experience. It has a basis in human experience. When
St. Paul says, as he does in the passage cited above,
that he is sure that nothing can separate us from
the love of God, he is speaking on the basis of his

previous experiences of the love of God and of the fact of love in human experience. As the psychiatrist Ira Progoff has pointed out, death may end a life, but it does not end a relationship.[1] Love is greater than death.

Hope is a fundamental phenomenon in human existence. The twelfth-century Cistercian monk Bernard of Clairvaux spoke of "Christian hope as the remedy of human need."[2] The great pioneer of psychoanalysis Sigmund Freud, in his analysis of what it means to be human, found wishing to be the basic source of the energy of life. In the understanding of the Buddha, who lived some twenty-five hundred years ago, desire (sometimes translated as craving) is the basic fact of human existence and the cause of human suffering for which the Buddha's teachings sought to offer a way out. Medical doctors speak of the need of a "will to live" on the part of their patients as a basic ingredient for recovery from an illness. Hope is another way of speaking of wishing, desire, or a will to live. It is basic to life.

In Christian tradition (following Paul's suggestion in the thirteenth chapter of First Corinthians), the three theological virtues are faith, hope, and love. We have been exploring love (which St. Paul called "the greatest") with all these road signs. Faith is often confused with believing in something impossible to believe, but as has been noted, faith in the New Testament means trust, a relying upon something. It is a matter of commitment, a virtue somewhat foreign to many today. Hope is also not always understood or valued.

Hope is a necessary ingredient in the kind of

prayer discussed in the chapter on "To Love Is to Offer." The creative imagination that we can offer is grounded in our previous experience of the matter concerned. That experience, however, may be a vicarious one rather than a direct experience. Hope provides the energy for seeing in our mind's eye God's purposes accomplished. Hope gives us the courage to undertake the journey into love. To love is to hope.

This road sign is also about what lies over the hill of life as we know it. Everyone knows that we are all going to die some day, but it has almost become a matter of bad taste to mention the fact. We think up all kinds of ways to say that someone has died or to avoid speaking of death. Until recently death had become almost a taboo subject in our society. The unreasonable reason for this is that we have resorted to a kind of primitive magic: trying to kill a fact by refusing to speak of it.

Human beings have always yearned for continuity of life, and in practically all parts of the world, in almost if not all religions, it is taught in one form or another. No one's life in this world is complete; no one here receives complete fulfillment. It is as though we were made for something more.

It is often assumed that the Christian church teaches the "immortality of the soul." Actually, it often does, thanks to the Greek philosophical tradition in which the writers of the New Testament and the early church fathers were nurtured. It also teaches something, however, that on the face of it is much more difficult—the resurrection of the body, one of the teachings, incidentally, in which Jesus agreed with the Pharisees of his day. Christian people, in common with others, normally have found immortality reasonable, and the idea of immortality is not especially in conflict with the Christian belief in resurrection. They are not the same, although they may be emphasizing two different aspects: the role of the created and the Creator, the human and the divine, works and grace.

Immortality implies that there is in humans a soul or something which is innately indestructible, eternity being of its very nature. Resurrection implies that God, by a gift, will raise up and continue in life the whole person, including a medium of being and expression, that is, a "body." In short, immortality is conceived in terms of nature; resurrection is to be conceived in terms of grace or gift. Immortality asserts an indestructible life for the soul; resurrection promises a recreated life for the whole personality. Obviously, it is not the same kind of "body" now known, as St. Paul points out in his letter to the early Christians in Corinth (1 Cor. 15). But it does suggest some kind of continuation of individuality. Immortality points to continuity; resurrection points to the necessity of relationship with God in order to have a new life in all its fullness of possibility.

The ancient Creed of the Christian church says, "I believe . . . in the resurrection of the body and the life everlasting." Christians have differed (even in New Testament writings) in their ideas about "the last things: heaven and hell."

A few years ago, my wife and I were struck in our reading by how many modern writers will give you a definition of "hell." The most striking contrast was this: Jean-Paul Sartre (an atheist) says in

No Exit: "Hell is other people." T. S. Eliot (a Christian) says in *The Cocktail Party*: "Hell is oneself." Both writers are speaking the truth as they see it. For Jean-Paul Sartre the world is without God; rather, freedom is enthroned as the supreme reality. The human is seen as an animal who chooses, who has freedom. Sartre does not know that for life one's choice is God—all he knows is the fact of freedom, our independence, and the self is what exercises this. So, of course, it is *other people* who infringe on one's freedom, and they are indeed "hell." (Though Sartre does not know it, it is also true, where God is in the picture, where Love is enthroned, that heaven too is other people.)

Eliot, the Christian, has one of the characters in *The Cocktail Party* say: "Why could I not walk out of my prison? What is hell?" And he goes on to answer it himself: "Hell is oneself, hell is alone, the other figures in it merely projections. There is nothing to escape from, and nothing to escape to. One is always alone." It is human self-assertion over against God which is hell. Hell is the self-willed separation from God. There has to be a hell. Hell is the necessary fact if there is freedom. (And freedom is the necessary soil for love to grow in.)

It is frequently asked, "How could a good God allow people thus to suffer?" The answer is that God has left us free, free either to center our lives on God or on ourselves. Each one of us is so free that we can devote all that we have or are to the work of God's kingdom, or neglect God's claim upon us and attempt to create a kingdom with ourselves as king. The first is heaven and the second is hell. Hell is not a place where people burn forever; it is much worse: it is self-willed separation from Love.

Can such separation from God be final? In principle, yes, or else there would be no real freedom. But when we come to think of how things will in fact work out, we must take into account our experience with God in this life, especially as we have come to know God in Jesus, the Christ. In one of the stories Jesus told, the Father is ever ready to come down the road and receive those who want to come home. Love accepts us just as we are. When you have been loved, you know that this is true.

Hope moves out from a present experience, yet leaps beyond what has already been experienced and moves into the future. In my experience of love in this life, I have ground for the conviction that God does not alter his relationship toward those who have died. My own experience tells me that death may end a life, but it does not end my relationship with the one who has died. Perhaps the choice remains with us; perhaps we can leave hell whenever we choose love.

One New Testament writer suggests that Christ preached the "good news" to all those who had lived before the time of God's coming in Jesus (1 Pet. 3:19). Most of the great theologians of the church have understood and taught that such an opportunity for response to God in Christ is required by our belief in God's justice, not to mention our faith in his mercy. One thing is certain, love never fails. If we make the journey into love, we are there. If we decline, love reigns without us. As in the parable of the wedding feast (Matt. 22:1–10), when the invited guests would not come, the banquet still went on; so the heavenly banquet will go on. To be absent from it is hell.

Heaven is being with God. Both heaven and hell are to be thought of as a state of existence, a relationship, not limited by space and time. I like to think of heaven as a pilgrimage to God. We are ever growing in our knowledge and love of God as pilgrims in this life, and so it seems, as we continue on the road over the hill, beyond death. An old prayer of the church asks that those who have "departed this life in thy faith and fear" may have "continual growth in thy love and service." Another prayer, for those who have died, asks "that they may go from strength to strength." There is the suggestion here of an intermediate state, as it has been called, when we finish that work which we begin when we choose God. St. Paul described the ultimate fulfillment as a "vision of God"—"For now we see through a glass, darkly; but then face to face" (1 Cor. 13:12).

To love is to hope. Because we experience God's love in this life, as we are "buried with Christ" in the death of our egocentered will, and "rise to newness of life" as his will becomes our will (as he becomes "our Lord")—*then*, because of our experience of this, we have confidence and hope and expectation that God's love for us continues beyond death. As we journey into love in this life, and experience God's love and grace (help), we are given hope and expectation that the road continues beyond the hill, over which we cannot see.

Down through the centuries, the distinctive act

of worship for the Christian church has been "the Lord's Supper," "the Mass," "the Eucharist," "the Holy Communion," "the breaking of bread"—by whatever name. In this service, we have a oneness with all God's people; those now and all those who have gone before.

In the Eucharist (the "thanksgiving"), it is as if a window in heaven is opened, and the Holy Table is a bridge reaching from this world into the eternal world and from the eternal world into this world. In this eucharistic action, all of God's creation joins in praise and worship and in thanksgiving for God's gift to us in creation. We are joined, as an ancient liturgy says, "with angels and archangels" and "with the whole company of heaven"—all those who have gone before.

In the Requiem Eucharist (that is, a Communion service marking the death or the remembrance of one who has died) it is as if the *passage* from one end of the table to the other is marked. But the one who has "departed," as we say, is still around the table of our Lord and joining in the praise and worship of him in a *new* way and yet an *old* way. At the Lord's Supper we are around the table once more, not only with all those here in this life, but with all faithful people everywhere, in this world and in the world to come. This, not the cemetery, but the altar of the church, is the place to be when we want to be near all those members of our own families when they have departed this life. This has been the faith of Christians ever since the first resurrection morn, when the Lord was known to two of his disciples in the "breaking of bread" (Luke

24:13–35). The Communion service is always a victory banquet. Love conquers all. When someone we love moves from one side of the holy table to the other, well do we sing: "The strife is o'er, the battle done, the victory of life is won; the song of triumph has begun, alleluia!"

To love is to hope.

9

To Love Is to Be Reborn

> Nicodemus said to him, "How can a man be born when he is old?"
>
> (John 3:4a)

For those who have begun to follow through on the journey into love, it is an experience of rebirth, of resurrection. That is the meaning of the greatest of the Christian festivals, Easter. While Christianity has hope "for a life to come," the Easter experience of being reborn begins in this life. There is a newness of life available now, the proclamation of which is the core of the "good news."

Why is it experienced as rebirth and called "being born again"? Not everyone who uses the term may think of it this way but psychology may tell us something about the psyche's experience that can well be described as being "reborn."

Birth entails some pain. Any new situation requires at least some adjustment to the new. Birth into the world entails a process of separation. In

speaking of psychological development Jung remarked: "There is no birth of consciousness without pain."[1]

Coming to consciousness means separating out
the thing of which one is becoming conscious from
that out of which it came, from its matrix, from
its "mother." This includes, of course, one's sense
of oneself—what psychology calls the ego. Thus it
is a necessary process. Yet what was appropriate
for the morning of life, following our birth and
"growing up," is no longer appropriate for the after-
noon of life. A change of perspective is required
in midlife, and the transition is not easy. People
try all kinds of things at this time—a new husband, a new wife, a new job, or perhaps a new way
of dressing. Unfortunately, Jung said, we have no
schools for adults. What seems to be required is
the establishment of a new relationship with life
itself. Instead of an outer journey, a moving into
the world and establishing one's place in it, the mature years call for an inner journey. In a sense, what
is called for is a reestablishment of a relationship
with what we have left behind. Such a restoration
is like starting over, like being reborn. One could
think of it as indeed a return to the womb out of
which one developed, but it is a return without
losing the accomplishment of consciousness. The
process of separation is ended; the journey into relationship begins.

Jung concluded that, given the opportunity, the
psyche heals itself just as the body heals itself (our
medicine only clears the way for the healing process
to take place). So also Jung came to the conclusion
that we are programed to seek a relationship with

something beyond the conscious ego. That "something" Jung chose to call the Self, a confusing term for many, for he meant something far beyond our usual idea of oneself. He spoke of the Self as the *imago dei*, that is, the image of God experienced within the psyche. In the achievement of consciousness the ego may be reluctant to give up any of its autonomy, but the pressure is there, manifested in different ways, outwardly and inwardly, for the ego to find its completion in something beyond itself. Jung believed the Self was behind this experience of longing on the part of the ego. This, of course, is like the conclusion of the mystics and spiritual writers through the ages and in all traditions. Augustine of Hippo said it all in his conclusion: our hearts are restless until they find their rest in God.

The journey of the ego in recovering a relationship on a more conscious level with that out of which it came is called by Jung, as has been noted, the path of individuation. In religious language it is a journey into love, into a relationship with God. To be reborn is to recover a relationship in a new way, with one's whole being, with others, and with God.

Meister Eckhart, the German Dominican friar (1260–*ca*. 1328), was a master at the University of Paris, a theologian, a seminary teacher, and a powerful preacher with a great gift with language. His central themes were the union of God and the human soul and the birth of the Son in the soul. Some of his contemporaries felt he went too far in speaking of the closeness of the relationship between God and the soul, although ever since Augustine of Hippo writers on the Christian experience had pointed to this relationship in various ways, and some contemporary historians think there was precedent in the church fathers for Eckhart's way of speaking. At any rate he was put on trial and eventually, after his death, some of his writings were condemned by Pope John XXII in 1329.[2] This fact has not diminished but may even have stimulated interest in Eckhart ever since.

It has been suggested by one historian that there are two types of mysticism in the history of Christianity. "One type stresses forms of extraordinary experiences, unique moments of conscious awareness of standing outside ourselves in union with God. Another type, the Eckhartian type, aims at penetrating the ordinary in order to reveal the extraordinary."[3] The latter type distrusts transitory experiences and seeks a new way of life. Eckhart called this "living without a why."

In his *The Counsels of Discernment* Eckhart warned that feelings are misleading and stressed that the inner being of God's love is more important than any sensed manifestation. Eckhart once said: "There are people who want to see God with the same eyes with which they look at a cow, and they want to love God the same way they love a cow . . . for the milk and the cheese."[4]

The language of rebirth was not foreign to Eckhart. In his commentary on John, Eckhart said, "As long as we are not like God and are still undergoing the birth by which Christ is formed in us (Ga. 4:19), like Martha (Lk. 10:41) we are restless and troubled about many things. But when Christ, God's Son, has been formed in us so that 'we are in his true Son' (1 Jn. 5:20) . . . 'we shall be like him, for we shall see him just as he is, having been made one in him and through him' (1 Jn. 3:2; Jn. 17:21)."[5] Then, Meister Eckhart adds, we shall be at rest as Augustine said.

Eckhart was deeply concerned with the individual's inner growth in the journey into love, but he also assumed that the committed Christian would be deeply engaged in the world, as he himself was. In his *The Counsels of Discernment*, he advises: "We ought not to think of building holiness upon action; we ought to build it upon a way of being, for it is not what we do that makes us holy, but we ought to make holy what we do. However holy the works may be, they do not, as works, make us at all holy, but as we are holy and have being, to that extent we make all our works holy, be it eating, sleeping, keeping vigil or whatever it may be."[6]

Good Friday followed by Easter symbolizes, in the Christian tradition, the victory over separation and the assurance of one's continuing relationship with God. The cross acts out God's love. We seem to need that. We may be told over and over (as Peter and the disciples were), but then we need to find the reality of that experience for ourselves. Peter found it, even after his denial when Jesus was arrested, in the forgiveness and acceptance he experienced in his encounter with his risen Lord.

The experience of rebirth is, of course, different for each person. As Eckhart said, "God does not work alike in every man's heart; he works as he finds willingness and receptivity."[7] None of the stories are the same, yet each in its own way describes an experience of joy and of new life. Living in this world is not an easy matter for most of us, I suspect.

It may appear so as we look at others, but seldom do we know, really, what life is like for them. The Easter message, with its promise of new life and acceptance, despite the worst that may have happened, is about a way out of the vortex of self-centeredness, that spiral which slides one down and down, round and round, until there is no concern outside of oneself. Well did Dante make the bottom ring of hell ice, in which there could be no movement, just frozen selves.

A much-admired woman once told her daughter-in-law: "The way to happiness lies in serving others." She knew from experience. She had read correctly one of the road signs that leads to eternal life now. She had found her vocation and the joy of new life. We must be careful, however, in giving advice to others; vocation is an individual thing. One person's calling is not necessarily another's. One must read carefully the road signs on the journey into love. In order to experience the joy of new life, our service of others must not involve laying a claim on their being, on their freedom, as the road sign about abandoning pride indicated. To be reborn requires an entry into love, a love that sets others free while maintaining a relationship. That is the emphasis in Al-Anon, the organization for members of the alcoholic's family. Jung once wrote one of his correspondents that no one could become aware of his individuality unless he was closely and responsibly related to his fellow human beings.[8] In a similar way, Teresa of Avila tested the reality of one's union with God (the goal of Christian spirituality) with whether it produced service to others.

When one is reborn, life falls into place; it is

a "centering" experience. Christianity is not alone in this emphasis on rebirth. Learning what life is about and what gives it meaning and value has been a goal in most of the world's religious symbol systems. Existence in the world for human beings has probably always meant, in various degrees and situations, some experience of anxiety, discouragement, fear of death, loneliness, and wonder at what it all means. In ancient times, people hoped to find some pattern in the stars that gave meaning and significance to daily life; for some, astrology still seems to function in this way. If this human yearning for meaning is not met, it apparently becomes a problem, as so much of the secular world indicates. The Austrian psychotherapist Viktor Frankl tells us that our basic problem is the search for meaning. Without that, life is empty and clouded with at least psychological ills.

Meaning is found, of course, in a variety of ways. For some it is providing the basic material needs of the family. For others, the primary value may be the building up of a business. Most people serve a number of values, all of which are important to them. At times one value has to be sacrificed in the service of another value. At times we may find the value we have been serving is unworthy of our service; our "god" may have deserted us.

Meaning is found, it seems, in being related to something outside oneself, something beyond one's ego-consciousness, as has been said. Being related to another human being in some way is of inestimable value in making the journey into love. It is best, of course, when this can be effected directly with another person, but it is possible through books.

Ultimately, love of things does not satisfy this need. Relationship to other life forms which may or may not respond seems to be a necessary experience to penetrating the mystery of love. It opens the door to our love relationship with God.

The psychologist Abraham Maslow suggested a hierarchy of needs of the individual. The basic needs generally have to be satisfied before one moves on to others. The list of needs is on an ascending scale:

1. physiological needs for survival
2. safety (security)
3. belongingness: to love and be loved by others
4. to experience some esteem by others
5. self-actualization

Obviously, the hierarchy of needs is not a rigid one; people vary in the order of their values. This is, however, the general pattern.

The importance of a relationship outside oneself can be seen in each of the needs on the list. In general, the priorities move from a relationship to material things to a relationship to other people and finally to a relationship with an intangible value involved in one's own being. Self-actualization, in Maslow's view, is not a self-centered or selfish stance toward life but, on the contrary, may well involve altruistic action to an extreme degree—such as laying down one's life for another. By self-actualization he means fulfilling what in religious language has been called one's "vocation."

The journey into love involves *knowing oneself*, as these road signs have suggested and as the wisdom of many cultures affirms. However, in knowing oneself one finds that there is a world beyond with which one must be in relationship if life is to seem worthwhile.

In speaking to a conference of pastors Jung once said something that has become perhaps his most quoted statement by people interested in religion:

> Among all my patients in the second half of life—that is to say, over thirty-five—there has not been one whose problem in the last resort was not that of finding a religious outlook on life. It is safe to say that every one of them fell ill because he had lost that which the living religions of every age have given to their followers, and none of them has been really healed who did not regain his religious outlook.[9]

Jung said he did not necessarily mean membership in a religious institution. Rather, he meant finding the "connection," that which relates the individual to something larger than him or herself, which gives significance and meaning and value to life. As we have noted in discussing Jung's path of individuation, what is involved in the journey is a moving beyond the ego and its concerns to something larger, to something that confronts the ego with demand. The ego must "bring the sacrifice" and when this is done, the resulting experience is one of rebirth. Much of Jung's writing is concerned with the variety of symbols with which this experience of rebirth is represented.

Throughout the history of Christian spirituality the journey into love has had, in various forms, some understanding of a union or reunion of the soul of the individual with God. The apostle Paul seems to have understood the goal as a seeing of God "face to face," though presumably this form of the experience would take place in the life to come as now we see only "through a glass darkly." However, Paul also understood God as present in the soul in some sense, as he speaks of our being "in Christ" and Christ dwelling "in us." Commentators have called this Paul's "Christ mysticism" (the "mystics" being those in the Christian tradition who have described the experience of a oneness with God). The charismatic movement that involves speaking in tongues is one expression of this desire and experience of a union with God—in this case, one human capacity, speech, is given over to the Holy Spirit of God.

In the history of Christian spirituality, the contact with God has, for many, been experienced as a vision. Francis of Assisi had many visions, the most memorable of which, with a profound effect on later Christian devotional practices, occurred in 1224, two years before his death. While in prayer on the mountain of La Verna he saw a six-winged seraph with the crucified Christ in the center. During this experience he received the stigmata—experiencing the five wounds of the crucified Christ in his own physical body. Francis also had auditory experiences, the first one of which led him into his ministry. While in prayer he heard a voice from the cross speak to him directing him to repair his church. At first, Francis responded literally and began repairing delapidated church buildings, but then he came to see the deeper meaning of building up the whole church which needed some "repair." Later in his ministry his associates report that he carried on dialogues with God while in prayer.

Whatever way God comes to us, when it happens, then we know. The danger has always been for Christians to say, "God is here—and *not* there!" What one affirms is generally more reliable than what one negates. The experience of God is an individual experience and others may or may not have the same experience.

The goal of the journey is to be at one with God. We may not necessarily experience this through the senses. For Augustine it was an experience of the mind, the intellect. There he found the evidence of God's presence.

However experienced, the goal of the Christian pilgrimage through life is a journey into love—a "love poured into our hearts," as Paul described it. According to John's gospel it was Jesus himself who taught his followers to look for and expect a presence of God in their inmost being when he was no longer with them in person.

The promise of new life now is the promise not only of Easter but also of Pentecost, the gift of the Spirit of God. To come into the kind of awareness that entails is like making a journey. It feels like being born again. The psyche is programed, as I have said, for spiritual growth just as the body is programed for its physiological development. There is a difference, however. Spiritual growth requires a choice, some conscious decision-making on our part. It is an adult task. Having obtained an identity, the task becomes one of recovering a relationship— with all parts of oneself, with others, and with God.

Not only are we programed for spiritual growth, the wisdom of the mystical traditions as well as contemporary psychological research also tell us we are programed for the possibility of a direct encounter, an immediate relationship, with God—if we are willing to undertake that journey, and life has provided the opportunity. The experience comes in a variety of ways as William James pointed out at the beginning of our century in his classic study of the psychology of religion, *The Varieties of Religious Experience*. However it is experienced, one finds that to journey into love is to be reborn.

Notes

Introduction

1. Victor and Edith Turner, *Image and Pilgrimage in Christian Culture* (Oxford: Basil Blackwell, 1978), p. 33.
2. Jean Dalby Clift and Wallace B. Clift, *Symbols of Transformation in Dreams* (New York: Crossroad, 1986); *The Hero Journey in Dreams* (New York: Crossroad, 1988).
3. Jolande Jacobi, *The Psychology of C. G. Jung*, trans. Ralph Manheim, 6th ed. rev. (London: Routledge and Kegan Paul, 1962), p. 59.

Chapter 1 / To Love Is to Grow

1. Huston Smith, Preface in *Meister Eckhart: The Essential Sermons, Commentaries, Treatises, and Defense*, trans. Edmund Colledge, O.S.A., and Bernard McGinn (New York: Paulist Press, 1981), p. xi.
2. Ibid.
3. Christopher Bryant, "The Nature of Spiritual Development," in *The Study of Spirituality*, ed. Cheslyn Jones, Geoffrey Wainwright, and Edward Yarnold, S.J. (New York: Oxford University Press, 1986), p. 565.
4. Walter Hilton, *The Ladder of Perfection*, quoted in F. C. Happold, *Mysticism: A Study and an Anthology* (Baltimore: Penguin Books, 1963, 1967), p. 287.
5. John Welch, a Carmelite, has provided a helpful contemporary reading of Teresa's vision in his study, *Spiritual Pilgrims: Carl Jung and Teresa of Avila* (New York: Paulist Press, 1982), where he uses Jung's psychology as an aid in exploring Teresa's images that portray the journey.
6. C. G. Jung, "The Stages of Life," in *The Collected Works*

of C. G. Jung, trans. R. F. C. Hull (New York: Pantheon Books, 1954), 8:387–403.

7. C. G. Jung, "The Meaning of Psychology for Modern Man," in *The Collected Works,* trans. R. F. C. Hull (New York: Pantheon Books, 1964), 10:149.

8. Quoted in Alan Jones, *Exploring Spiritual Direction: An Essay on Christian Friendship* (New York: The Seabury Press, 1982), p. 123.

Chapter 3 / To Love Is to Abandon Pride

1. Benedicta Ward, "The New Orders," in *The Study of Spirituality,* ed. Cheslyn Jones, Geoffrey Wainwright, and Edward Yarnold, S.J. (New York: Oxford University Press, 1986), pp. 287–88.

2. F. C. Happold, *Mysticism: A Study and an Anthology* (Baltimore: Penguin Books, 1963, 1967), p. 205.

3. Jean Leclercq, O.S.B., Introduction in *Bernard of Clairvaux: Selected Works,* trans. G. R. Evans (New York: Paulist Press, 1987), p. 38.

4. Ibid., pp. 39–40.

5. Happold, *Mysticism,* p. 211.

6. J. B. Phillips, *When God Was Man* (New York and Nashville: Abingdon Press, 1955), pp. 26–27.

7. Ibid., p. 27.

8. C. G. Jung, *Two Essays on Analytical Psychology,* in *Collected Works,* trans. R. F. C. Hull, 2d ed. rev. (New York: Pantheon Books, 1966), 7:156, n. 1.

9. Edward Edinger, *Ego and Archetype* (New York: G. P. Putnam's Sons, 1972), p. 15.

10. C. S. Lewis, *Christian Behavior* (New York: Macmillan Company, 1950), p. 44.

11. Bernard of Clairvaux, "On Humility and Pride," in *Bernard of Clairvaux: Selected Works,* p. 103.

12. Lewis, *Christian Behavior,* p. 47.